Elizabeth Barrett Browning and the Poetry of Love

Nineteenth-Century Studies

Elizabeth Barrett Browning and the Poetry of Love

by
Glennis Stephenson

U·M·I Research Press
Ann Arbor / London

Copyright © 1989
Glennis Stephenson
All rights reserved

Produced and distributed by
UMI Research Press
an imprint of
University Microfilms Inc.
Ann Arbor, Michigan 48106

Library of Congress Cataloging in Publication Data

Stephenson, Glennis, 1955-
  Elizabeth Barrett Browning and the poetry of love / by Glennis
Stephenson.
    p. cm—(Nineteenth-century studies)
    Bibliography: p.
    Includes index.
    ISBN 0-8357-1977-4 (alk. paper)
    1. Browning, Elizabeth Barrett, 1806-1861—Criticism and
interpretation. 2. Love poetry, English—History and criticism.
I. Title. II. Series: Nineteenth-century studies (Ann Arbor, Mich.)
PR4197.L65S74   1989
821'.8—dc19   89-4697
                                                         CIP

British Library CIP data is available.

To my parents

Contents

Acknowledgments

I would like to thank Rowland McMaster, Sara Stambaugh, Audrey Andrews, and Judith Fisher for their help and advice. To the University of Alberta and the Social Sciences and Humanities Research Council of Canada I am grateful for their financial support. Thanks are due to John Stasny and Paul Kenny for allowing me to reprint material previously published in *Victorian Poetry* and *Browning Society Notes.* And finally, and most importantly, thanks to Juliet McMaster for everything.

1

Introduction

In 1932, Virginia Woolf began an unsuccessful attempt to revive interest in the works of Elizabeth Barrett Browning with a bleak appraisal of the extent to which the poet's reputation had declined:

> By one of those ironies of fashion that might have amused the Brownings themselves, it seems likely that they are now far better known in the flesh than they have ever been in the spirit. Passionate lovers, in curls and side whiskers, oppressed, defiant, eloping—in this guise thousands of people must know and love the Brownings who have never read a line of their poetry. . . . "Lady Geraldine's Courtship" is glanced at perhaps by two professors in American universities once a year; but we all know how Miss Barrett lay on her sofa; how she escaped from the dark house in Wimpole Street one September morning; how she met health and happiness, and Robert Browning in the church around the corner.[1]

The romantic and sentimental view of Barrett Browning so vividly captured in these lines has, until quite recently, kept a firm hold on both the popular and the literary imagination. Long after Browning's reputation as a poet had been established, Barrett Browning's fame continued to rest on the role that she played in the most celebrated of Victorian love stories. Woolf's judgment on her position as writer remained true: "Nobody reads her, nobody discusses her, nobody troubles to put her in her place."[2] The poetry was overshadowed by the looming image of the romantic heroine in ringlets, the delicate invalid with the pale spiritual face and the dark intense eyes who escaped from the tyranny of a monstrous father when she was carried off to Italy by her dashing poet-lover.

The manner in which Barrett Browning's works were read during the late nineteenth and early twentieth centuries had much to do with establishing her as personality rather than as poet. She was considered mainly as the writer of love letters and sonnets to her husband, and the effusive idolatry of such commentators as Lilian Whiting (1899) and Louise Boas (1930), along with the patronizing approval of Eric Robertson (1883) and Osbert Burdett (1928), contributed little to an understanding of the works. As their interest was confined to the ways in which the poetry and correspondence could be seen to reveal the womanly love experienced by the author, critics and biographers only strengthened and elaborated on the image of the romantic heroine which had first begun to emerge during Barrett Browning's lifetime.

Many recent feminist critics have reacted strongly against this view of Barrett Browning, and in their reassessments of her poetry she has emerged as an intellectual woman with strong interests in political and social reform. *Aurora Leigh*—hailed by Ellen Moers as *"the* feminist poem"[3] and now seen as her most significant work—has secured her an important place among nine-teenth-century writers. The numerous articles published on Barrett Browning's work since about 1975 focus primarily on *Aurora Leigh,* or deal with social and poetic questions raised by *Aurora Leigh* in the more general context of other works. It is surely telling that the *Sonnets from the Portuguese,* once so highly esteemed, is often ignored. While critics have done much to improve Barrett Browning's reputation by exploring her social and political concerns, and by considering such questions as the relationship of genre and gender and the position of the woman as poet, they have also shown an unfortunate tendency to shy away from discussing Barrett Browning as a poet of love. The romantic ballads and lyrics are usually forgotten, and the sonnets uneasily dismissed.[4]

The apparent unwillingness of critics to approach Barrett Browning on the subject of love may be partly attributable to a fear of invoking the oppressive specter of ringlets and "Robert Browning in the church around the corner," which continues to haunt the popular, if not the literary, imagination. Barrett Browning as romantic heroine obviously retains an appeal for many: flowery editions of the *Sonnets from the Portuguese* still find a place on the shelves of local bookshops, and lines from the sonnets and love letters still turn up each year, usually around February, in greeting cards. The degree to which Barrett Browning continues to epitomize romantic love is graphically demonstrated by a recent Canada Post advertisement which exploits and merges the sonnets and the letters. A dreamy-eyed teenage girl is depicted holding an envelope appar-ently addressed to the rather wild-looking young rock star (the poet Browning's twentieth-century avatar?) whose picture stands framed beside her. Super-scribed above the girl's head is the immortal line: "How shall I mail this? Let me count the ways."

Rather than being freed from the romantic myths which grew up around her, Barrett Browning may be in the process of splitting into two distinct personalities: the serious intellectual poet reclaimed by the academic world, and the sentimental love poet abandoned to the masses. The morbid fear of becom-ing associated with sentimentality has led to a regrettable critical neglect of the emotional content of Barrett Browning's works. But while sentimentality is certainly a distinguishing feature of the myths, it is hardly characteristic of the love poetry: the poems often exploit and undermine the sentimental, but they rarely *indulge* in it.

Barrett Browning's poems of and about love generally have little to do with the romantic myths or her actual romantic experiences. Even when these experiences do exert an influence on her art, in *Sonnets from the Portuguese,* she does not provide what earlier critics assumed that they found in the poems—the unmediated expression of the author's own womanly love. Instead, she skillfully adapts and transforms her personal situation in order to produce particular dramatic effects. As love poet, Barrett Browning has far more in common with the intellectual reclaimed by the critics than with the almost mythic figure of the heroine in ringlets. The main interest of her love poems lies in the ways in which they are influenced by, and concerned with, the social, cultural, and poetic conventions regarding women and love.

Barrett Browning explores two major issues in her poems of and about love: the question of woman's role in love relationships and the question of woman's voice in love poetry. In both these areas, she accepts and also resists the prevailing patriarchal traditions. She does not romanticize the life of the single woman or advocate the repression or rejection of sexual desire. Nor does she envision the possibility of fulfillment being found in a separate community of women; "sisterhood" is never posited as a satisfying alternative to a happy marriage. Barrett Browning believes in the importance of romantic love. She does, however, insist that the traditional form of male-female relationship must be modified in order to allow women to assume an active, functional, and fulfilling role.

Similarly, although she was notably concerned by the lack of a female poetic tradition, Barrett Browning nevertheless closely identified with the established male tradition and was not prepared to reject it entirely. The love poetry documents her struggle to find a place within this tradition which would allow for the forceful expression of the female lyric voice of desire. In this respect, her major contribution towards the formation of a female tradition lies in her attempts to adapt the conventional forms and situations used by her male predecessors and her female contemporaries, and in her efforts to provide the woman, previously confined to the role of the silent beloved, with a strong and passionate voice.

The nature of Barrett Browning's achievement as a love poet can be best appreciated when her work is viewed against the background of early nineteenth-century women's poetry. Love is certainly the most popular subject for the numerous women poets who began to write at the beginning of the century, and yet, somewhat paradoxically, love poetry presented the women with more problems than any other form of verse. These problems had much to do with the lack of an established female tradition. "England has had many learned women, not merely readers but writers of the learned languages, in Elizabeth's time and afterwards," Barrett Browning observed in her much-quoted complaint to Henry Chorley, and yet where were the poetesses? The divine breath which seemed to come and go, and, ere it went, filled the land with that crowd of true poets whom we call the old dramatists—why did it never pass, even in the lyrical form, over the lips of a woman? How strange! And can we deny that it was so? I look everywhere for grandmothers and see none. It is not in the filial spirit I am deficient, I do assure you—witness my reverent love of the grandfathers![5]

A woman attempting to give expression to the female lyric voice of desire found the absence of such a tradition particularly troubling. In the conventional romantic lyric, first established and developed by Petrarch, the subject or active "I" is masculine; the object of desire, silent and passive, is feminine; and the plot enacted is the masculine plot of distance and desire: the suffering male eloquently describes the remote lady and the experience of love while the pursued female usually remains aloof or indifferent—and always silent. She is highly idealized by the speaker, and, in the most extreme cases, becomes an abstract, almost allegorical figure, an angelic, even dead, spiritual guide.

While the plot and characters established by Petrarchan convention do not account for all romantic lyrics, they do dominate the male amatory tradition. The pleading, questing man, torn between hope and despair, is the archetypal lover of the lyric, and it is this character who serves to give expression to male desire, over and over again, in the works of such poets as Sidney, Spenser, Donne, Keats, and Shelley. The very existence of a strong opposing tradition, exemplified by Shakespeare's "My mistress' eyes are nothing like the sun" and appropriated by Rochester, Suckling, Swift, and many others, only testifies further to the wide-spread influence of the original.

In her study of the rhetoric of sexuality in Dickinson and Rossetti, Margaret Homans observes that women writers did not often choose to write conventional love lyrics; to do so was either "to repeat the traditional quest plot, in linguistic drag, or to take up the position of the silent object and attempt to speak from there."[6] Only Christina Rossetti, in her "Monna Innominata," was interested enough to speculate at length about what that silent object might have said if she had been allowed to speak. Laura, Beatrice, Stella, and all the other traditional types do not, understandably, seem to have held much appeal for the woman attempting to establish her position as a love poet.

In the early decades of the century, women generally responded to the problems posed by the romantic lyric by devoting most of their energy to writing poems *about* love, poems in which the gender of the narrator is rarely specified and becomes relatively unimportant; ballads and romance-narratives became their most favored forms. Poetry *of* love, the lyrical expression of the emotion and the type of verse which traditionally excluded women from the role of speaking subject, was approached, if at all, with much trepidation.

This tendency to lean towards the narrative or descriptive rather than the lyrical is evident in the works of both Felicia Hemans (1793–1835) and Letitia

Landon (1802–35). By far the most popular and influential women poets during the first few decades of the nineteenth century, Hemans and Landon were primarily responsible for the establishment and early development of what is now often called the female sentimental tradition. Barrett Browning's thorough acquaintance with their works—and the works of numerous other long-forgotten women poets—is clearly confirmed by the frequent references to their poetry in her correspondence, and their works provide useful representative examples of those conventions governing women's poetry with which Barrett Browning was familiar.

Although Hemans is usually associated with the domestic affections, it is surprisingly difficult to find anything amongst her works that can with complete conviction be described as a short love lyric giving expression to woman's passion or desire. Even in those poems she labels songs or lyrics, Hemans leans more towards the narrative or the descriptive. She is evidently far more comfortable telling stories about love than attempting to give expression to the emotions of love. Only her *Translations from Camoens and Other Poets* (1818) falls decisively within a lyric tradition, and, adopting the voice of the male lover, Hemans here proves herself quite proficient in the use of the sonnet. But while she skillfully uses the love sonnet to give voice to the traditional male speaker, and while she exploits the sonnet form to write of religious, historical, and patriotic themes—she even writes sonnets on "Thoughts during Sickness"—Hemans rather tellingly makes no attempt to adapt the form to accommodate the female lyric voice of desire.

This is not to suggest that women do not speak in Hemans's poems. She contributed much towards developing the form of the female monologue, and the absence of any distinctive female lyric voice is all the more striking for the profusion of women's voices which tell us about the fate of their love in her narratives and monologues. These voices sound most assertively and compellingly in *Records of Women* (1828). While Hemans sometimes declares in her brief introductions to these poems her intention of giving expression to women's "thoughts and feelings,"[7] this series of narratives and monologues actually confirms that, as Dolores Rosenblum notes, Hemans "is not especially interested in exploring psychological states; rather she focuses on types and typifying occasions."[8]

"Prosperzia Rossi," with its depiction of another woman artist's attempt to give expression to desire, provides an apt illustration of Hemans's own characteristic method of dealing with love. Unable to declare her unrequited love in any other manner, Rossi sculpts a bas-relief of the forsaken Ariadne. This character becomes the mold into which she pours all her desire—"the fervent thoughts, the untold, / The self-consuming" (277). Rossi's hope is that after her own death, all her grief and passion will finally be communicated to the man she has loved through the sculpture of Ariadne in her most characteristic pose, lamenting by the lonely sea.

Like Rossi, Hemans gives expression to the female lyric voice of desire by creating types of female devotion—women who reveal love by what they do rather than by what they say. In "Gertrude, or Fidelity till Death," the woman proves the extent of her love by remaining at her husband's side while he slowly dies in agony on the wheel. Unable to save him, she still manages to give some comfort and is rewarded for her own heroic endurance by one last smile. The abandoned Costanza reveals the depths of her still perfect love when, as her false lover, wounded in battle, returns to die in her arms, she can tenderly hold him to her "wronged bosom" and declare "I live / To say my heart hath bled, and can forgive" (303). Juana, wife of Philip of Austria, is completely ignored by her husband, but when he dies she patiently watches his corpse, convinced he will revive and smile on her at last; "years of hope deferred," she believes, would be repaid "by one fond glance of thine" (299). For all Hemans's women, love is "more / Than fiery song may breathe, deep thought explore" (267); the extent of their affection can be shown only through action, through patient devotion, endurance, and suffering.

Ideal love, Hemans-style, is a wifely, domesticated love which is character-ized primarily by deep friendship and self-sacrifice. In spite of the extravagance of their acts of devotion, her women often appear emotionally restrained; "O gentle, gentle friend" (267), "my lost friend ... my soul's friend" (326) are some of their typical endearments. No matter how exotic the setting or charac-ter she describes, Hemans's women usually sound suspiciously like middle-class English wives. Their relationships would be more correctly described as com-fortable than as passionate. Hemans is, as Barrett Browning observed, perhaps "too obviously a *lady*,"[9] and her poems of love are marked by that "conventional excess of delicacy which was the flaw in her fine genius" (MRM 2.371).

A more flamboyant and fiery love can be found in Landon's works. There is a sense of rawness in the feelings Landon tries to depict, a suggestion of sexual passion which makes her poems far more erotic than those of Hemans. Since she does not write many of the short verses of the type Hemans labeled songs or lyrics and usually prefers extended narratives or monologues, Landon may, at first glance, appear to avoid the lyrical even more than Hemans. But Landon generally interpolates songs and lyrics into her long verse, and the manner in which her women express love is actually more suggestive of the emotional life than Hemans's emphasis on story, action, and typifying stances.

Landon also wrote of a female artist—her Improvisatrice—who creates an Ariadne in the hope that her beloved may someday "think—see—feel all I felt, in this memorial."[10] The difference between the ways Landon and Hemans treat Ariadne points up the main distinction between their methods of giving expres-sion to woman's love. For Hemans, the characteristic stance—the woman lamenting by the sea—suffices; further detail is unnecessary and her Ariadne is, above all, a type of female devotion. For Landon, the specific details of Ariadne's appearance are of far more importance. Her Improvisatrice draws a picture suggestive of the deserted woman's anguish:

> Her black hair loose, and sprinkled o'er
> With white sea-foam;—her arms were bare,
> Flung upwards in their last despair.
> Her naked feet the pebbles prest;
> The tempest-wind sang in her vest;
> A wild stare in her glassy eyes;
> White lips, as parched by their hot sighs;
> And cheek more pallid than the spray
> Which, cold and colorless, on it lay.

(1.47)

In Landon's poems, woman's love is most frequently revealed through expressions and displays of extreme anguish and despair. The conventional signs of grief become indicative of the depths of passion, and Landon repeatedly dwells on physical appearance, physical responses, to suggest fierce emotion. The tale of love, as she writes in *The Golden Violet* (1826), is expressed most clearly by tangible evidence of the "woman's creed of suffering": "Her eye may grow dim, her cheek may grow pale, / But tell they not both the same fond tale?" (1.206).

While Hemans and Landon differ slightly in their approaches to the presentation of love, they, along with all other contemporary female poets, consistently agree on one important point: they almost always associate woman's love with sorrow—usually the result of either the death or the inconstancy of the beloved. They seem as incapable of writing about happy love as Landon's Improvisatrice:

> I touch'd my lute,—it would not waken,
> Save to old songs of sorrowing—
>   Of hope betrayed—of hearts forsaken—
> Each lay of lighter feeling slept.
> I sang, but, as I sang, I wept.

(1.19)

The emphasis on "old songs of sorrow" becomes unfortunately limiting. As the Petrarchan and anti-Petrarchan traditions developed, the male love poet managed to dramatize a variety of states of mind: "Shall I compare thee to a summer's day?" "When by thy scorn, O murderess, I am dead," and "Loving in truth, and fain in verse my love to show" may share their origins in the same tradition, but they share little else. The female love poet, far more restricted in her choice of topic and her mode of expression, continually returns to the single situation of the despairing woman and her grief. And as Barrett Browning observed of Landon, "the striking of one note does not make a melody" (MRM 1.18).

Why these poets so repeatedly associate woman's love with sorrow can only be a matter of speculation; they provide little in the way of explanation themselves. Landon does often claim that woman's constancy and man's fickleness are innate qualities, but this does not entirely explain her emphasis on unhappy love; when her male characters *are* loyal, she usually disposes of them rather quickly and leaves her women to mourn their untimely deaths. The implication seems to be that inconstancy and death are, in themselves, of relatively little consequence—they function primarily as means by which the women can be placed in the desired state of despair.

Part of the explanation for the association of woman's love and sorrow may lie, quite simply, in the area of technique. A woman unhappy in love does not need to say much. Grief can lead to silence or to expressions of sorrow rather than to declarations of desire. The language of love can be replaced by the language of grief, or continuing love can be expressed through acts of devotion or endurance. The problems the woman poet faces constructing a subject capable of voicing lyric female desire are not solved, but avoided. Happy love is perhaps less easily suggested by action and appearance; it tends to call for more direct and vocal expression.

There is also the question of decorum. Women were simply not supposed to take the initiative in love, and while descriptions of the continuing love of a deserted maiden were conventionally acceptable, bold confessions of a lusty lady's fancies and her appreciation of her lover's physical charms were not. Unhappy love provides the poets with the best possible situation in which to depict women fulfilling their most idealized and conventional role in relationships—the role of passive suffering and noble endurance. And one of the most striking points about both Hemans and Landon is their willingness to accept the female mask, to act out the roles traditionally assigned to women in both art and life.[11] Not only do they impose the mask and roles on their fictional female characters, but they also, in their own characters of women poets, impose the mask and roles upon themselves.

While Hemans wrote on quite a variety of subjects, she never attempted any topic that her audience might consider unsuitable for a woman poet. Landon chose to limit herself even further and focused almost exclusively on love. In the preface to *The Venetian Bracelet* (1829), she explains this decision:

I can only say, that for a woman, whose influence and whose sphere must be in the affections, what subject can be more fitting than one which it is her peculiar province to refine, spiritualize, and exalt?[12]

Landon's choice of "Love as my source of song"[13] should not be too hastily attributed to a "romantic" nature; by addressing her audience in this fashion she reveals herself to be an astute businesswoman. Much of her popularity, as Rosenblum notes, was the result of "her eagerness to convey that she was not intruding upon masculine territory;"[14] women poets were expected to confine themselves to women's subjects, and Landon took pains to point out that she was doing exactly what her audience required of her.

And while they continually suggest that love brings women only unhappiness, both Landon and Hemans stress their acceptance of the female mask by nevertheless insisting that love is still by far the most important thing in woman's life. Fame, in comparison, they claim to be of little consequence. There is no struggle in their works of the kind found in Barrett Browning's *Aurora Leigh*, only an absolute acceptance of the primacy of love. As she busily produces volume after volume and competently supports herself and five children, Hemans continues to declare: "Thou hast a charmed cup, O Fame! / Away! to me—a woman—bring / Sweet waters from affection's spring" (465). And her Prosperzia Rossi agrees:

> Give the drooping vine
> Something round which its tendrils may entwine—
> Give the parched flower a raindrop, and the meed
> Of love's kind words to woman! Worthless fame!
>
> (278)

Landon, who creates many strong female artist figures, similarly diminishes as she exemplifies woman's ambition and achievement: "My power was but a woman's power" claims her Improvisatrice (1.2); "I am a woman:—tell me not of fame" says Eulalie in "The History of the Lyre" (2.52). Landon and Hemans, both prolific and successful poets, accept the rules of the game they have chosen to play: for a woman, they insist, the actual activity—writing—is far less important than the subject—love.

Their acceptance of the conventional female role is also suggested by the nature and the situation of the women they choose to depict. These women are continually placed—by their unhappy experiences in love—in situations where they can reveal their devotion and their capacity for passive endurance. Hemans's Madeline, a girl who loses her husband, her "bosom's first beloved, her friend and guide" (304), on her wedding-day, may be too young to play her role correctly, but Hemans can still seize the opportunity to emphasize the lesson which must be learned:

> the part
> Which life will teach—to suffer and be still,
> And with submissive love to count the flowers

Which yet are spared, and through the future hours
To send no busy dream!

(304–5)

Neither Hemans nor Landon shows any overt signs of rebellion concerning woman's fate in romantic relationships. Landon even claims that there is little reason to complain since man's fate is equally bleak; his

most golden dreams of pride and power
Are vain as any woman-dreams of love;
Both end in weary brow and wither'd heart,
And the grave closes over those whose hopes
Have lain there long before.

(2.227)

But while Landon and Hemans willingly assume the female mask and convey their acceptance of the female role, by repeatedly juxtaposing the notion that woman's love is always unhappy with the idea that woman's role in romantic relationships is one of passive endurance, they often indirectly suggest that unhappiness in love may in some sense be related to the restrictions of the passive role. The possible link between the two is at least implied by Hemans's "Evening Prayer at a Girls' School." Gazing upon the schoolgirls at prayer, Hemans sees in the youthful happiness of the "joyous creatures" the seeds of both woman's tenderness and woman's woe:

Her lot is on you—silent tears to weep,
    And patient smiles to wear through suffering's hour,
And sumless riches, from affection's deep,
    To pour on broken reeds—a wasted shower!
And to make them idols, and to find them clay,
And to bewail that worship,—therefore pray!

Her lot is on you—to be found untired,
    Watching the stars out by the bed of pain,
With a pale cheek, and yet a brow inspired,
    And a true heart of hope, though hope be vain;
Meekly to bear with wrong, to cheer decay,
And oh! to love through all things,—therefore pray!

(403)

It is difficult to determine whether Hemans considers the inevitable unhappiness of women to be caused primarily by the actions of others or by the necessity of enduring, meekly, patiently, and silently, the consequences of those actions. The only solution that she offers, in either case, is "therefore pray." The final tone is one of acceptance. Neither Hemans nor Landon shows any overt signs of rebellion and neither makes the connection between woman's unhappiness and woman's restricted role directly.

In Barrett Browning's many comments upon the works of Landon and Hemans, it is their willingness to bend to convention to which she most often objects. While Hemans's work is pronounced regrettably ladylike, constrained by an excess of delicacy, Landon's genius is considered "not strong enough to assert itself in truth." It *"suffered* her to belie herself—and stood by, while she put on the mask;" as a result, a "conventional tone pierces through the sweetness" of her poetry (MRM 1.232–33). It was left to Barrett Browning to reject that mask and to announce, in a loud and decidedly unladylike voice, that the time had come for a rigorous reappraisal of the conventions—both those which silenced woman's voice in love poetry and those which restricted woman's role in romantic relationships.

Early Ballads and Lyrics: The Pains of Love

"The earthly good of this world," Barrett Browning wrote to Mary Russell Mitford in 1837, "is its happiness; and its happiness, like its sorrow, issues from its affections" (MRM 1.27). It is the pains and problems of love, however, not its delights, that Barrett Browning dwells upon most frequently in the early ballads and lyrics. In poem after poem, relationships fail, love ends in death or betrayal, and the protagonist—nearly always female—is left to find what consolation she can in the arms of God. By so consistently associating love, and particularly women's love, with sorrow, Barrett Browning places herself firmly within the female sentimental tradition.

She is not, however, simply catering to popular taste or following an established convention; the position she adopts in her poetry closely reflects the opinions to be found in her correspondence. Love in the abstract was undeniably important to her—"Life is dreary indeed without love," she claimed in 1841, "the sand were not worth the footsteps" (MRM 1.268)—but she was at best ambivalent about experiencing the emotion. She even told R. H. Horne that since pain was invariably associated with the affections, she once considered that she would, given the chance, avoid knowing anyone she was likely to love or be loved by intensely.[1] Love *might* bring joy—she was certain that it would bring sorrow.

The desire to avoid possible unhappiness by choosing withdrawal from, rather than engagement with, the world is frequently expressed in Barrett Browning's correspondence, and her dissatisfaction with love appears to be only part of a general dissatisfaction with life itself. Various griefs and illnesses during her early years led her to crave tranquility. "I can't understand the craving for excitement. Mine is for repose," she told Mary Russell Mitford in 1839:

My conversion into *quietism* might be attained without much preaching, and, indeed, all my favorite passages in the Holy Scriptures are those which express and promise peace. . . . They strike upon the disquieted earth with such a *foreignness* of heavenly music—surely the "variety," the *change,* is to be unexcited, to find a silence and a calm in the midst of thoughts and feelings given to be too turbulent. (MRM 1.110)

Much of her correspondence with Mitford, however, reveals a quite different personality, a woman with a lively, gossipy interest in the world around her, and particularly in the romances of her acquaintances. It is not surprising, therefore, that her desire for withdrawal from the world is matched by a conflicting and equally strong desire to experience the life from which she was in so many ways excluded—and a clear awareness that her poetry suffered from her isolation: "where a poet has been shut off from most of the outward aspects of life," she wrote to Browning, "he is at a lamentable disadvantage."[2]

Torn between the desire for withdrawal from and engagement with life, Barrett Browning reveals that she has as much in common with her male as her female contemporaries. She appears in many respects as the embodiment of a Lady of Shalott, both attracted and repelled by the spectacle of life and the prospect of involvement. These counter-impulses are variously dramatized throughout many of the early ballads and lyrics, and exert a considerable influence on Barrett Browning's presentation of love.

A desire to withdraw from the world is predictably expressed most frequently and most simply in the early religious verse of the 1833 and 1838 volumes. "Idols" and "The Sleep" provide useful examples of this position; both poems focus upon contrasting man's love with God's, and the failure of earthly love to match up to divine appears to be the major cause of the desire for withdrawal.

In "Idols," the speaker disparagingly dismisses human affection when reflecting upon the three weak gods of this world that she has worshipped. Beauty fades, and Fame soon seems cold and comfortless; both of these earthly gods betray her trust. Human Love, however, proves to be far the worst:

> Last, human Love, thy Lares greeting,
>   To rest and warmth I vow'd my years.
> To rest? how wild my pulse is beating!
>   To warmth? ah me! my burning tears.
>
> Ay! *they* may burn—though thou be frozen
>   By death, and changes wint'ring on!
> Fame—Beauty!—idols madly chosen—
>   Were yet of gold; but *thou* are STONE![3]

Since this human Love fails her, she refuses to lament its loss:

> Crumble like stone! my voice no longer
>   Shall wail their names, who silent be:

> There is a voice that soundeth stronger—
> "My daughter, give thine heart to *me!*"
>
>   (1.161)

Only by giving her heart to God, the father-lover who "deathless love in death declarest," will she find happiness, she concludes: "None else is beauteous—famous—dear!" (1.161). The overly dramatic pauses, the abundance of exclamations, and the insistent emphasis in "Idols" result in the speaker's rejection of love being much too frantic to be convincing; she does not seem to have accepted the failure of earthly love quite as completely or as easily as she would have us believe.

God and death in these early poems frequently appear to be little more than an escape, a convenient and peaceful refuge from the disappointments of the world. With a somewhat adolescent morbidity, the unhappy cry of "Weariness," "I would—I would, I were at rest" (1.163), echoes throughout the religious lyrics, and the longing for that "land of rest deferr'd" becomes a simple desire to avoid further conflict and sorrow through embracing death (1.163).

"The Sleep," a poem prompted by one of Barrett Browning's favorite biblical passages, avoids the almost frenzied tone which marks such works as "Idols" and "Weariness," and concentrates instead on attempting to capture the mesmerizing attraction of that final peaceful rest. Comparing God's gifts with man's, the speaker asks:

> What do we give to our beloved?
> A little faith all undisproved,
> A little dust to overweep,
>
> . . . .
>
> "Sleep soft, beloved!" we sometimes say,
> Who have no tune to charm away
> Sad dreams that through the eyelids creep:
> But never doleful dream again
> Shall break the happy slumber when
> He giveth His belovèd—sleep.
>
>   (2.88)

Despite the melodic beauty of the refrain, "He giveth His belovèd—sleep," or perhaps because of it, the poem is somewhat disturbing; the heavenly land of rest where God soothes the dead with his sweet music bears a discomfiting resemblance to the land of the Lotus eaters. The suggestion of regressive infantile desire in "The Sleep" is further emphasized by the speaker's characterization of herself as a child in need of the comfort and security that God alone appears able to provide:

> For me, my heart that erst did go
> Most like a tired child at a show
> That sees through tears the mummers leap,
> Would now its wearied vision close,
> Would childlike on His love repose
> Who giveth His belovèd—sleep.

(2.88)

Barret Browning may be using the image of the child only in a conventional religious manner in this poem, but in other works she will begin to use the same image to suggest the naivety of those who seek a solution to all problems in simple withdrawal and retreat.

It is the gradual movement towards using the image in such a manner that makes "Isobel's Child" of some interest. This is not one of Barrett Browning's more successful pieces—she is rarely at her best describing mothers and babies—but the poem is not quite as artless and sentimental as it may first appear. Isobel's baby is dying, and as she nurses him through the night she prays for God to spare his life. Her prayers are answered, and his fever and pain disappear. The child is far from grateful. Straining the reader's credulity past the limit, Barrett Browning has the child become suddenly capable of eloquent speech and world-weary reason; the little prodigy calls upon his mother to "loose" the prayer which so cruelly binds him to earth. After seeing heaven and God's "love-large eye" in his dreams, he has no desire to remain on the "dark" and "dull / Low earth" (2.24); human love holds not the slightest appeal:

> Love! earth's love! and *can* we love
> Fixedly where all things move?
> Can the sinning love each other?
>   Mother, mother,
> I tremble in thy close embrace,
> I feel thy tears adown my face,
>   Thy prayers do keep me out of bliss—
> O dreary earthly love!
> Loose they prayer and let me go.

(2.27)

It would surely be wrong to assume that the child speaks for Barrett Browning; the poem as a whole does not reject human love quite as unequivocally as this passage might suggest. The child is, after all, rather a special case; he is destined to die and has already had a taste of what lies ahead. As the nurse's dream of the poplars on the hill clasping the setting sun until it "waned and paled" implies (2.11), Isobel's prayer interferes with the natural order of things; after seeing heaven, the child would only pine away if forced to remain on earth. More importantly, however, the child's pessimistic appraisal of human love is thoroughly contradicted by Isobel's actions; in changing her prayer and allowing the child to die, she reveals a most selfless perfect love. It is only the child, this seems to suggest, with a naive view of good and evil, who is incapable of recognizing the true value of earthly love.

A quite different position is dramatized in another early religious work, "The Seraphim." There is a decided preference for the troubles of earth over the perfections of heaven in this poem, and Barrett Browning begins to explore the doctrine of the glory of the imperfect that she—no less than Browning—will continue to develop. Witnessing the crucifixion, the seraphim Zerah and Ador recognize that man, sinful yet redeemed, will be capable of far greater love for God than the sinless seraphim with their finite perfection. In complete contrast to Isobel's baby, Zerah concludes: "Heaven is dull, / Mine Ador, to man's earth" (1.90).

In the early works which are concerned more particularly with romantic love, the dramatization of conflicting impulses towards withdrawal from and engagement with the world receives its most complex treatment in the companion pieces "A Poet's Vow" and "The Romaunt of Margret." The former, Barrett Browning wrote in her preface to *The Seraphim and Other Poems*, was intended to show "that the creature cannot be *isolated* from the creature"; the latter, "that the creature cannot be *sustained* by the creature" (1.68).

The poet in "The Poet's Vow," much like the soul in Tennyson's "The Palace of Art," decides to break the bondage which ties him to his fellow men in an attempt to dissociate himself from human sin. He determines to live alone in his ancestral hall and to return to a pre-lapsarian state of peaceful innocence in complete harmony with Nature; the deep love expressed by the silences and soft unseen looks of earth, sky, and seas, he believes, will be infinitely more satisfying than the changing love of his fellow men—to whom he obviously considers himself far superior. Responding to the remonstrances of his friend Sir Roland, he displays a most offensive pride:

> Go, *man*, to love! I go to live
> In Courland hall, alone:
> The bats along the ceilings cling,
> The lizards in the floors do run,
> And storms and years have worn and reft
> The stain by human builders left
> In working at the stone.
>
> (1.217)

As the contemptuous emphasis on *"man"* suggests, the poet no longer sees himself as part of the lowly human race; the only place for him is where the despicable stain of this race has been erased by the eroding, cleansing forces of the natural world. But only the "self-poised God may dwell alone," the narrator observes; even

> God's chief angel waiteth for
> A brother's voice, to sing;
> And a lonely creature of sinful nature
> It is an awful thing.

(1.217)

The poet soon becomes lonely and fearful—and as stagnant as the hall in which he sits. Indifferent to his fellow men and incapable of experiencing love or hate, joy or pain, he achieves only a cold, calm impassivity. He seems indeed too calm to be gentle in this troubled world where even the "very star that shines from far / Shines trembling ne'ertheless" (1.207). Nothing moves him until the death of Rosalind, the woman to whom he was betrothed and whom he heartlessly rejected when he made his vow. Rosalind has arranged for her corpse to be delivered to the poet's door accompanied by a scroll. "I left thee last, a child at heart, / A woman scarce in years," the message on the scroll begins:

> I come to thee, a solemn corpse
> Which neither feels nor fears.
> I have no breath to use in sighs;
> They laid the dead-weights on mine eyes
> To seal them safe from tears.

(1.223)

The pointed echoes of Wordsworth's Lucy in this passage have been noted by Dorothy Mermin.[4] Like Lucy, Rosalind is now an unfeeling thing; as a part of the poet's much-beloved earth, she can no longer be moved by mankind, only by the rotation of the globe. The corpse is silent, stiff, and chill: "No farther wrong, no farther woe / Hath license from the sin below / Its tranquil heart to thrill" (1.224). Rosalind can finally look upon the poet as dispassionately as he last looked upon her. The poet now realizes that the earth and sky which he has worshipped have also looked upon him "indifferently" (1.225); he has received no comfort, no joy, from his isolated existence.

Although "The Poet's Vow" reveals an advance on the over-simplified views put forward in such works as "Idols," the poem unfortunately suffers from Barrett Browning's tendency, as she put it, to *take every means to say what I think*" (RB 1.9). The lesson is too pointedly and too frequently forced upon the attention of the reader. With repeated descriptions of smiling friends and happy families, various images of hearts leaping together, branches entwining, angels singing in unison, and wood-doves nodding together in the trees, as well as such numerous narratorial aphorisms as "a lonely creature of sinful nature / It is an awful thing" (1.217), Barrett Browning ensures that the reader cannot fail to grasp the main point of the poem. Then, in the final lines, she still feels the necessity of spelling out the lesson in the baldest terms. As Sir Roland stands over the double grave of the poet and Rosalind, he admonishes his son for being too concerned with the natural world around him:

> Nay, boy, look downward, . . .
> Upon this human dust asleep.
> And hold it in thy constant ken
> That God's own unity compresses
>   (One into one) the human many,
> And that his everlastingness is
>   The bond that is not loosed by any:
> That thou and I this law must keep,
>   If not in love, in sorrow then,—
>   Though smiling not like other men,
> Still, like them we must weep.
>
>   (1.226)

The companion piece to this poem, "The Romaunt of Margret," is far more effective in its suggestiveness than "The Poet's Vow" with its direct and insistent emphasis upon a moral lesson. While Margret sits by the river, her shadow emerges from the water, sits by her side, and tells her that she must die unless she can name one person in the world who loves her as "truly as the sun" (2.4). After recovering from her fright, Margret is initially quite confident:

> "Can earth be dry of streams,
>   Or hearts of love?" she said;
> "Who doubteth love, can know not love:
>   He is already dead."
>
>   (2.4)

As she names each member of her family and finally her lover, Margret's confidence is slowly destroyed: her family is only interested in what she can do for them, and her one true lover is dead. Her gradual disillusionment is eerily reflected in the progressive deterioration of the world around her: the river stops flowing, the foliage on the trees withers, and the moon and stars fade from the sky; a chill silence descends on the earth, and Margret drowns herself.

The encounter described in the "Romaunt of Margret" is, as Dorothy Mermin observes, a "self-encounter."[5] Doubts concerning the love of others leads to psychic fragmentation; the doubting side—the shadow on her life and on the river—forces a confrontation to resolve the split. The trusting side is unfortunately too reliant upon the love of others for a sense of self, a sense of identity; as Barrett Browning notes, "the creature cannot be *sustained* by the creature." Margret has dedicated her entire life to pleasing and serving others, to winning their affection. Consequently, when the trusting side is convinced that the love she depends upon so completely is non-existent, the self is destroyed.

The poem concludes with the narrator's mournful summary:

> Hang up my harp again!
> I have no voice for song.
> Not song but wail, and mourners pale,
> Not bards, to love belong.
> O failing human love!
> O light, by darkness known!
> O false, the while thou treadest earth!
> O deaf beneath the stone!
>
> (2.10)

While the narrator, in an attempt to extract a lesson from the story he relates, appears to resolve the issue on the side of the shadow, we are left with the impression that this final summary somewhat over-simplifies an issue which has been shown to be far more complex in the preceeding stanzas. To begin with, the shadowy double is hardly presented in a manner likely to inspire much trust. Indeed, it is the embodiment of *distrust,* and appears as a truly malevolent force. Each time Margret finds out that she is not loved as she thought, the shadow responds with malicious glee and trembles on the grass with "a low, shadowy laughter" (2.5). This shadowy distrust depends for its existence on its ability to eat away Margret's confident self:

> My lips do need thy breath,
> My lips do need thy smile,
> And my pallid eyne, that light in thine
> Which met the stars erewhile.
>
> (2.4)

It is Margret's growing mistrust of human love and her tendency to rely too much on that love for a sense of identity—rather than the actual failure of love—which eventually destroy her.

Although it would appear an important point in favor of a more optimistic appraisal of human love that Margret's one true lover is not faithless, only dead, many of Barrett Browning's early poems suggest that the finite quality of earthly love has much to do with its inferiority to divine love. The perspective on death found in such poems as "The Romaunt of Margret" and "The Poet's Vow" is quite different from the perspective on death found in "The Sleep." While the idea of death as a happy slumber undisturbed by doleful dreams is a source of comfort and reassurance in the early religious poems, in the romantic ballads it is a cause of much misery. If the dead are undisturbed by human passion, their love for those left behind must end. Barrett Browning's resulting ambivalence becomes quite clear as she attempts to reason through her conflicting responses to Jung-Stilling's theory of a conscious and immediate spirit world:

> My feeling is that when our beloved go from us, *The beloved*, he who is so to God and man by right of title, stands there in the chasm. . . . Our dead are our absent ones!—and if as Stilling thinks their spiritual abode be in the midst of us, it is not less a state of separation,—and our cry, (happily for that new blessed peace they have won) cannot more reach and wound them. How can they hear any cry of ours?—Does death invest them with ubiquity—with omniscience—with God's own attributes?—or are they forced to walk step by step with us—they in their divine sympathy, and we in our earthly sorrowfulness—the one rent by the other?—No—it is not reasonable, I think, that we should wish it—nor is it scriptural that we should believe it. . . . Let us not wish to trouble the new peace of our dead. (MRM 1.315–16)

The many questions, qualifications, and hesitations in this passage are telling; Barrett Browning is clearly drawn in two directions.

Instead of dwelling on the comforts of death, the romantic ballads dwell upon its horrors. Death is shown to erect an impenetrable barrier between the living and the dead, and Barrett Browning vividly captures the appalling sense of void and separation by dwelling on the state of the body rather than the spirit. Rosalind in "The Poet's Vow" becomes an unloving corpse, and her message to the poet focuses on alienation and on the body's chill and unresponsive stiffness. And in "The Romaunt of Margret," the shadow relentlessly forces Margret to come to terms with the death of her lover with a delightfully grisly description of his rotting corpse:

> He *loved* but only thee!
>   *That* love is transient too.
> The wild hawk's bill doth dabble still
>   I' the mouth that vowed thee true:
>   Will he open his dull eyes
>   When tears fall on his brow?
> Behold, the death-worm to his heart
>   Is a nearer thing than *thou.*

(2.9)

That corpse which is gradually disintegrating into the earth has little to do with Margret's one true love.

A gradual change in Barrett Browning's attitude towards the subject of life after death can be traced in her letters to Mitford. When Mitford's father died, Barrett Browning's attempts to comfort her friend suggest that she was no longer certain that the dead did remain free from all troubling emotion. "It is over," she wrote, "the suffering of your beloved one—and now it is for *him*—(IF the sense of human tribulation *be* permitted to reach the delivered spirits)—it is for *him* to lean over *you* pityingly and tenderly" (MRM 2.116). The qualification is admittedly emphatic—Barrett Browning underlines IF three times—but in light of the situation, the very presence of the proviso shows her tentative new opinions were honestly considered, and not simply offered out of a desire to comfort her friend. By the time she published *Poems* (1844), Barrett Browning obviously believed that love did survive death. In the lyric "Loved Once," she suggests that human love has the potential to be, like divine love, never-ending; it only fails when man "desecrates the eternal God-word Love / By his No More, and Once" (3.108). True love, she adamantly declares, "strikes one hour—LOVE! Those *never* loved / Who dream that they loved ONCE" (3.110). Even after death, love continues:

> When life is shriven
> And death's full joy is given,—
> Of those who sit and love you up in heaven
> Say not "We loved them once."
>
> (3.109)

She is now convinced that there "comes no change to justify that change" (3.109), and although this cannot mitigate the pain of loss, it does elevate human love, in this respect, to the level of the divine.

Since Barrett Browning believed that love could and should last forever, she had little patience with the fickle. R. H. Horne, whom she greatly admired, was angrily denounced when she learned of his multiple amatory dalliances. "I acknowledge at once and unhesitatingly," she wrote to Mitford, "that the man who could throw his love from one woman to another,—has a love, worth no more than a cotton handkerchief, to throw. In such a case there could be no pure love—no pure sensibility" (MRM 2.409). But the belief that love "cannot by a law of its own nature pass away, die away, as is the manner of mortal things," she admitted upon another occasion, was a favorite dream: "do not speak loudly and wake me from it" (MRM 1.162). Ideally, she believed, human love should be as permanent and unvariable as divine love; practically, she recognized, it rarely is.

And as the companion pieces "A Man's Requirements" and "A Woman's Shortcomings" reveal, the prime offender is man.[6] The monologue spoken by the self-centered gentleman of "A Man's Requirements" initially appears to suggest that the poem is a relatively light-hearted attack on the belief that men will inevitably stray and women doggedly love on. The speaker describes to his sweetheart exactly what he expects from her in their relationship:

> Love me, Sweet, with all thou art,
>   Feeling, thinking, seeing;
> Love me in the lightest part,
>   Love me in full being.

(3.206)

After ten stanzas of insistently demanding "Love me"s, in which the speaker expounds the necessity for a full and frank surrender, the poem ends with a cynical twist as the cocksure Romeo announces what he can offer in return:

> Thus if thou wilt prove me, Dear,
>   Woman's love no fable,
> I will love *thee*—half a year—
>   As a man is able.

(3.208)

Barrett Browning may seem to be suggesting, tongue in cheek, that the speaker has simply found a highly convenient excuse for taking so much and giving so little. It is also possible, however, that the prevailing tone is finally bitter rather than light-hearted, that Barrett Browning believes this *is* all man can offer.

The ambiguous "A Woman's Shortcomings" simultaneously contradicts and supports the second reading. This lyric focuses on a flirtatious woman who is unwilling to commit herself to one man and prefers to bask in the attentions of many (women can clearly trifle with men's affections too). Thoughtlessly, she flits from the gentleman serenading her outside to the gentleman praising her inside and freely bestows her smiles upon both. The disapproving narrator reprimands her with a lesson in the true nature of love:

> Unless you can think, when the song is done,
>   No other is soft in the rhythm;
> Unless you can feel, when left by One,
>   That all men else go with him;
> Unless you can know, when unpraised by his breath,
>   That your beauty itself wants proving;
> Unless you can swear, "For life, for death!"—
>   Oh, fear to call it loving!

(3.206)

Once again, however, the poem ends with a cynical twist as Barrett Browning undercuts this prescription for loving:

> Unless you can dream that his faith is fast,
>   Through behoving and unbehoving;

Unless you can *die* when the dream is past—
Oh, never call it loving!

(3.206)

Barrett Browning's attitude towards love has clearly changed, even if her belief that it brings sorrow has remained relatively constant. The ideal of a permanent love might be just an illusion, a dream that will surely pass, but love now seems so important that she is nevertheless ready to insist upon the necessity of having faith in its absolute truth. Sexual betrayal, therefore, becomes a troubling theme to which she will continually return throughout her poetic career.

Barrett Browning's beliefs and doubts concerning love and her related conflicting desires for withdrawal from and engagement with life receive their most thorough treatment in a highly fanciful romance ballad entitled "The Lay of the Brown Rosary." The complexity of this poem has been underestimated, perhaps because Barrett Browning herself tended to devalue this and all other ballads she wrote to order for *Findens' Tableaux.*[7] Barrett Browning was obviously amusing herself with "The Lay of the Brown Rosary," and the ballad is full of outrageous Gothic devices; nevertheless, in spite of these extravagances, the poem addresses some serious and complex issues.[8]

Onora, the heroine of this supernatural tale, is waiting for the return of her lover from battle when she learns that she is destined to die—a fate which she can avoid only by vowing to renounce God. Choosing life in order to marry her betrothed, Onora makes her pact with the ghostly nun of the brown rosary. She becomes guilty of bartering God's love for man's and is soon punished; her new husband falls dead at the alter. In the last section of the poem Onora bewails the very human tendency to seek God only when earthly happiness is gone, and is finally allowed to die.

Onora's final lament appears to suggest that the point of the poem is simply to show her mistake in choosing a "love-lit hearth, instead of love and heaven,— / A single rose, for a rose-tree which beareth seven time seven" (2.274). But "The Lay of the Brown Rosary" actually reveals that Onora's choice is not as simple as it might originally appear. The poem begins by setting up a relatively straightforward series of distinctions between the forces of good and evil. The forces of good, those who would encourage Onora to withdraw from the world, to choose God's love and forego man's, find their most outspoken advocate in Onora's young brother. Unable to lie at all effectively (he is even incapable of coming up with a credible alternative to the truth when his mother quizzes him on Onora's whereabouts—and he blushes horribly) the young brother is the embodiment of purity and innocence. He is determined to expose his wicked sister, and he does not rest until she is suitably punished. For the naive child, the world is painted black and white, and the right choice, the right path, is always clear. The young brother's heavenly supporting cast includes the angelic forces and St. Agnes, who, in this poem, seems important primarily for her notoriety as a most determined virgin; the patron saint of all virgins, she rejected numerous suitors and consecrated her body to Christ—obviously the sort of thing God expects of Onora. Her function as the saint who gives young girls visions of their future husbands is not forgotten, however, and the interesting ambiguity inherent in her figure—virginity and consummation—is certainly significant in light of the ambiguities which develop in the poem.

Ranged against these forces of good are miscellaneous shrieking fiends and the chilling ghost of a nun. The nun has a ghastly brown rosary, a "string of antique beads, / By charnel lichens overgrown" (2.256); she is associated with all the horrors of the night and more particularly, as the young boy tells his mother, with:

> The old convent ruin the ivy rots off,
> Where the owl hoots by day and the toad is sun-proof,
> Where no singing-birds build and the trees gaunt and grey
> As in stormy sea-coasts appear blasted one way.
>
> (2.256)

Initially, therefore, the poem might suggest that in being forced to choose between divine and human love, Onora must simply choose between good and evil, God and Satan. An important dream sequence, however, reveals that the decision which she must make is actually far more complex.

While Onora sleeps, she dreams that she is a child again, happily walking hand in hand with her dead father—and, by implication, with God the father—through the fields beneath the autumn sun. The ghostly nun appears at her bedside demanding "Forbear that dream—forbear that dream! too near to heaven it leaned" (2.260). Onora is puzzled; she has vowed "*I would not thank God in my weal, nor seek God in my woe*" (2.265), and the dream, she responds in her sleep, is "most innocent of good":

> It doth the Devil no harm, sweet fiend! it cannot if it would.
> I say in it no holy hymn, I do no holy work,
> I scarcely hear the sabbath-bell that chimeth from the kirk."
>
> (2.260–61)

But Onora is wrong in assuming the dream to be "innocent of good"; in this world, the innocent *is* the good.

The nun is not just the representative of the devil with a mission to tempt Onora to reject God, she is also the representative of the loss of innocence, of adult sexuality. She was buried alive for her sins, the traditional penalty doled out to those who broke vows of chastity. While the figure of the nun is usually associated with total withdrawal from the world, this particular nun chose man's love over God's, sexuality over innocence, and died unrepentant, an inverted Agnes, shrieking curses which kill an old abbess and suggest the disruptive power of adult sexuality.

One of the initially confusing aspects of this poem is that Onora was consorting with the nun before the fateful choice was forced upon her. The point must be important, since Barrett Browning went to the trouble of adding this particular angle when she revised the poem for publication in *Poems* (1844). In the original version of 1840 in *Findens' Tableaux*, Lenora, as the heroine is initially called, first meets the nun when the ghostly figure appears and tells her that she is destined to die, a fate which she can avoid only by renouncing God.[9] In the 1844 text, Onora has been meeting the nun prior to learning of her fate, and the information comes not from the evil spirit, but from God's angels. The revision is slight, but important. It ensures that the reader does not doubt that it is God who forces Onora to choose between divine and human love. In the original version it remains possible that the girl is tricked by the evil spirits. Furthermore, the revision suggests that Onora's growing awareness of adult sexuality—signified by her association with the nun—might be the reason that God forces her to make the choice.[10] His insistence on Onora's choosing between human and divine love in the original version seems quite arbitrary and rather senseless. The choice, indeed, may now be seen as a kind of test administered by a divine but jealous lover. As she begins to find value in human love and is no longer simply content with the divine, Barrett Browning may be registering some guilty sense of betrayal.

When Onora must choose between God and man, therefore, she must choose not simply between good and evil, or withdrawal from and engagement with the world, she must also choose more particularly between eternal innocence and sexual maturity. God's hold over her is threatened by her growing sexual desire; the nun's by her conflicting regressive fear of sexuality and a Peter Pan desire never to grow up. It is the innocent purity of childhood found in Onora's dream which the nun fears, and this purity must be defiled: Onora must repeat the vow in the presence of her ghostly father.

The call of the father, "Come forth, my daughter, my beloved, and walk the fields with me!" (2.261), is not initially entirely rejected by Onora. In her dream she explains her predicament:

> I wish I were a young dead child and had thy company!
> I wish I lay beside thy feet, a buried three-year child,
> And wearing only a kiss of thine upon my lips that smiled!
> The linden tree that covers thee might so have shadowed twain,
> For death itself I did not fear—'tis love that makes the pain.

(2.262–63)

Lying under the linden tree, the tree of conjugal love, Onora would be joined with her father in a non-sexual marriage; she would remain a child forever—and a dead child at that. The father's call is a call to death and duty; like God, with whom he basically merges, he prefers Onora to choose death and innocence over life and sexual maturity. (I will refrain from making the almost inevitable inference about the relationship of Elizabeth and Mr. Barrett.)

Onora, however, is not a child; to this full-grown woman eternal innocence is not such an appealing proposition:

> I was no child, I was betrothed that day;
> I wore a troth-kiss on my lips I could not give away.
> How could I bear to lie content and still beneath a stone,
> And feel mine own betrothed go by—alas! no more mine own—
> Go leading by in wedding pomp some lovely lady brave,
> With cheeks that blushed as red as rose, while mine were white in grave?
>
> (2.263)

Death itself, Onora explains, she does not fear, but "Love feareth death" (2.263). The phrase needs some qualification. For the adult woman with knowledge of mature romantic love, the choice between withdrawal from and engagement with life can never be as simple as it is for a child. It is not just human love in general which complicates the choice (love for her mother or brother apparently would not have stopped Onora from embracing death); it is romantic love in particular that becomes disruptive, that finally prevents man from being content with God's love alone.

In the ballads which follow "The Lay of the Brown Rosary," the idea that the steadfast love of God will always amply compensate for the failure of earthly love still occasionally emerges, but the assurance becomes less and less convincing and is generally placed in the mouths of characters of questionable authority. In "Rhyme of the Duchess May" the narrator's support for this point of view is a clear indication that he has misunderstood the moral of the story that he reads. This romance ballad is divided into three main sections. The first contains the narrator's description of himself sitting beneath a willow tree in a churchyard, surrounded by graves and listening to the church bells toll for the dead. In this far from cheery setting, he reads the ancient rhyme which comprises the second section of the poem. The story concerns Duchess May, an orphan whose guardian, her uncle, has betrothed her to his son Lord Leigh. May refuses to marry her churlish cousin and elopes with the man she loves, Sir Guy of Linteged. Three months later, the castle of Linteged is about to fall into the vengeful hands of Lord Leigh. Sir Guy concludes that only his own death will avert further catastrophe and decides to make a grand gesture and ride off the castle wall; his remaining friends will surely then be spared, he believes, and his wife soon reconciled to her cousin. May refuses to let him die alone, and, despite his horrified protestations, jumps on the horse just as it plunges off the castle wall. Finally, the last section of the poem returns to the doom and gloom of the narrator as he attempts to extract a suitable moral from the story he has read.

The poem is built on a series of contrasts which reflect the story's central preoccupation with the opposing forces of life and death: the energetic rhythm with its alternating anapests and paeons is repeatedly interrupted by the slow, funereal pace of the refrain "Toll slowly"; the noises of life—the rustling leaves and rushing river—are placed against the sounds of death—the tolling church bell; the morbid passivity of the narrator is contrasted with the energetic willfulness of the woman whose tale he reads; and, most importantly, the excitement of the adventure is offset by the deathly stillness of the setting in which it is told.

Having read the rhyme, the narrator notices in the churchyard the grave of a three-year-old child, Maud, and this leads him to ruminate on the fate of the willful lovers:[11]

> Though in passion ye would dash, with a blind and heavy crash—
> *Toll slowly*—
> Up against the thick-bossed shield of God's judgement in the field,—
> Though your heart and brain were rash,—
>
> Now your will is all unwilled; now, your pulses are all stilled:
> *Toll slowly.*
> Now, ye lie as meek and mild (whereso laid) as Maud the child
> Whose small grave was lately filled.
>
> (3.27)

"Beating heart and burning brow" are now calm as the corpses patiently await Resurrection (3.28), and the contrast of this calm with the lively song of the birds overhead prompts the narrator to reflect: "All our life is mixed with death, / And who knowest which is best?" (3.28).

The answer favored by the narrator becomes obvious when, with evident satisfaction, he concludes,

> Oh, the little birds sang east, and the little birds sang west—
> *Toll slowly.*
> And I smiled to think God's greatness flowed around our incompleteness,—
> Round our restlessness, His rest.
>
> (3.28–29)

The narrator may prefer the meekness of Maud to the passion of May, and the peacefulness of death to the turmoil of life, but Duchess May's energy, defiance, and determination to find happiness in love are presented in such an attractive light that it becomes impossible to accept the inference that her passion was wasted and meaningless or that the culmination of life is this impassivity. Compared to her initial energy, May's eventual dispassionate peace seems only torpid apathy.

In the early religious poems, to withdraw from the world, to embrace God and "childlike on His love repose" (2.88), may seem to be an attractive proposition, but the romantic ballads soon challenge the idea that God's love alone can provide happiness. God is, perhaps inevitably, a rather cold and distant figure in these poems, certainly not a satisfactory substitute for the human lover. Earthly life and earthly love are shown to be the source of sorrow as well as joy, but they still eventually appear preferable to the perfect placidity of heaven and divine love. It is not so difficult to sympathize with Onora's fateful choice of a "love-lit hearth, instead of love and heaven."

Love and Marriage: The Roles of Women

Although Barrett Browning soon began to emphasize the importance of human love, she retained many reservations about the romantic relationship in its traditional form. The ideal marriage would be based on a "fulness of sympathy, and a sharing of life, one with another" (RB 2.957), she believed, but her observations of contemporary society led her to conclude that such an ideal was seldom realized. Describing her feelings prior to meeting Browning, she remembered that a "happy marriage was the happiest condition, I believed vaguely— but *where were the happy marriages?*" (MRM 3.189). From the frequency with which the subject appears in her poetry and correspondence, it would seem that she considered the main obstacle to the attainment of the "happiest condition" to be the socially and culturally established limitations placed upon women in romantic relationships. There could be no "fulness of sympathy" as long as women were restricted to a narrow domestic sphere, and when women were chosen for wives, they were certainly not chosen as companions:

> When they are selected to be loved, it is quite apart from life—"man's love is of man's life a thing apart." A German professor selects a woman who can merely stew prunes—not because stewing prunes and reading Proclus make a delightful harmony, but because he wants his prunes stewed for him and chooses to read Proclus by himself. . . . Men like to come home and find a blazing fire and a smiling face and an hour of relaxation. Their serious thoughts, and earnest aims in life, they like to keep on one side. And this is the carrying out of love and marriage almost everywhere in the world—and this, the degrading of women by both. (RB 2.957)

In such medieval ballads as "Rhyme of the Duchess May" and "The Romaunt of the Page," Barrett Browning dramatizes the contemporary views of male and female roles and suggests how they reflect chivalric conventions.[12]

The noble knights in these poems may not be concerned with culinary skills, but they are as determined as the German professor to keep their women firmly planted in a stifling domestic world while they get on with "man's work" alone. Sir Hubert in "The Romaunt of the Page" is Barrett Browning's most outspoken advocate of the separate spheres theory. His wife, whom he has seen only once, disguises herself as a page in order to accompany him to Palestine—a fanciful idea perhaps prompted by the youthful Barrett Browning's determination to "dress up in men's clothes as soon as ever I was free of the nursery, and go into the world 'to seek my fortune,'" preferably as "poor Lord Byron's PAGE" (MRM 2.7). After saving her husband's life three times, the young woman attempts to determine how Sir Hubert would respond to her deception by fabricating a story about her sister following her husband as a page and fighting by his side. Sir Hubert is thoroughly amused by this absurd tale; his lady, he declares, does not belong on a battlefield:

> Well done it were for thy sistèr,
>   Thou tellest well her tale!
> But for my lady, she shall pray
>   I' the kirk of Nydesdale.
> Not dread for me but love for me
>   Shall make my lady pale;
> No casque shall hide her woman's tear—
> It shall have room to trickle clear
>   Behind her woman's veil.

(2.249)

The knight never pauses to consider the magnitude of the love and loyalty which would lead a woman to act in this manner; he simply dismisses such behavior as unseemly and concludes that he could never love anyone so "unwomaned" (2.248). "Look up," he tells his disguised bride,

> There is a small bright cloud
> Alone amid the skies!
> So high, so pure, and so apart,
> A woman's honour lies.

(2.249)

This chivalric view of woman's role in love relationships may superficially seem more romantically appealing than the prosaic views of the imaginary professor with a penchant for prunes, but Barrett Browning was well aware that the essential point was the same. Her disdain for both cloud-minding and prune-stewing was clearly revealed when George Barrett Hunter, an Independent Chapel minister and Barrett Browning's would-be suitor, presumed to apply his "romantic" principles to her. Barrett Browning was furious with the hapless Hunter who, significantly, spoke much the same language as her page's lout of a husband. "Ever since my last book has brought me a little more before the public," she complained with bitter indignation,

> I can do or say or wish to do and say, nothing right with him—and on, on, he talks epigrams about the sin and shame of those divine angels, called women, daring to tread in the dust of a multitude, when they ought to be minding their clouds. . . . You know...and I tell him,...the feeling is all to be analysed into contempt of the sex. It is just that, and no less. For a woman to hang down her head like a lily through life, and 'die of a rose in aromatic pain' at her death,...to sit or lounge as in a Book of Beauty, and be 'defended' by the strong and mighty thinkers on all sides of her,...this, he thinks, is her destiny and glory. It is not the pudding-making and stocking-darning theory—it is more graceful and picturesque. But the *significance* is precisely the same,—and the absurdity of a hundred times over, greater. Who makes my pudding is useful to me,—but who looks languishing in a Book of Beauty, is good for nothing *so far*. (MRM 3.81)[13]

Though Barrett Browning attributes Hunter's attitudes solely to "contempt of the sex," her indignant complaint nevertheless suggests that this contempt is somewhat paradoxically mixed with a sizable dose of anxiety; while men scornfully devalue the abilities of women as a group, she implies, they can still feel threatened by the accomplishments of a woman as an individual.

The origins of this uneasy fusion of contempt and anxiety are first described by Barrett Browning in the fragment of an "Essay on Woman" written during her teens. In this poem, which reveals the strong influence of Mary Wollstonecraft, Barrett Browning begins by wondering why woman has been neglected by the poets.[14] Traditional feminine concerns, "the hours of bliss domestic" and "Love's aerial dream," are not suitable subjects for poetry: "not for this the breathing lyre rebounds, / It wakes to loftier, more exalted sounds." As mother, sister, and wife, woman is prized for qualities indicative of weakness—timid smiles, tears, blushes, and trembling voices—and Barrett Browning wants to "bend to nobler thoughts the British fair":

> Can Woman only triumph in the sigh,
> The smile coquetish, or bewitching eye?
> Are charming words, and affectatious airs
> The only claim or notice that are hers?
> Are vases only prised because they break?
> Then why must woman to be loved be weak?

The blame for woman's deplorable condition is placed firmly on man's shoulders; "is this alone thy pride," she continues, to

> Smother each flash of intellectual fire,
> And bid Ambition's noblest throb expire?

Pinion the wing, that yearns for glory's light,
Then boast the strength of thy superior flight?

After eliminating all competition from women, Barrett Browning concludes, man is then free to "fetter, scorn, disdain" and "enslave" the woman who smiles submissively on his breast.[15]

The contempt of the sex to which Barrett Browning refers certainly underlies the "careless laugh" of Sir Hubert in "The Romaunt of the Page" when, with an offensive mixture of condescension and skepticism, he dismisses his wife's tale with "Well done it were for thy sistèr, / But not for my ladye!" (2.248). It is more explicitly shown, however—and is far more troubling—in "Rhyme of the Duchess May." Sir Hubert was compelled to marry and is none too happy about it, so perhaps some of his insensitivity is understandable, even though not forgivable. Of Sir Guy, who marries for love, more is expected. Guy's fear that he may be unable to protect his wife has obviously caused him much anxiety about his "manliness": when the castle is about to fall and prospects look dismal, there is a particularly telling moment when he leans upon his sword, and it shivers and snaps. To regain his sense of strength, dignity, and manliness, Guy decides to "die nobly for them all" (3.13), to prevent further bloodshed by sacrificing himself and riding off the castle wall on his horse. When May announces her determination to accompany him on this final ride, Guy only laughs. "Get thee from this strife," he orders, "In this hour I stand in need of my noble red-roan steed, / But no more of my noble wife" (3.21). Although May has previously provided him with ample evidence of her daring and courage, Guy persists in viewing her as though she were a weak and frightened child. After his death, he believes, she will soon be comforted by his enemies; like Sir Hubert, he associates women primarily with tears and prayers:

She will weep her woman's tears, she will pray her woman's prayers—
Toll slowly
But her heart is young in pain, and her hopes will spring again
By the suntime of her years.

(3.15)

Guy is painting a wholly inaccurate portrait of his willful wife; he is not taking her individual qualities into consideration, but simply endowing her with those traits he believes to be characteristic of women as a sex. When May claims the right to join him in his grand show-stopping exit, he is horrified; woman's role, he insists, is simply to weep and pray and be protected.

The two wives in "Rhyme of the Duchess May" and "The Romaunt of the Page" emphatically reject their husbands' limited views of woman's role in love and marriage. A wife should take an active role in the relationship and share all the trials, the "page" argues, and she repeatedly declares her conviction that her "sister's" behavior was truly womanly. Duchess May similarly insists on her right to share all aspects of her husband's life—and death—and, like the page, claims that this is womanly behavior. When Guy orders her away, she refuses to go: "Meekly have I done all thy biddings under sun," she reminds him, "But by all my womanhood, which is proved so, true and good, / I will never do this one" (3.21).

In these early poems dealing with the frustration which occurs when women are denied an active role, there is a telling lack of sensuous language and imagery in the description of romantic relationships. "Rhyme of the Duchess May" is particularly interesting in this respect, since May's sensuous nature is revealed nearly everywhere save in her relationship with Guy. There is even a notable, if rather disturbing, sizzle in her responses to the villainous Lord Leigh—perhaps because he treats her more like a worthy antagonist than a weak child. When Leigh shouts out his threats to her from beneath the castle walls, May calls in her maids to comb out her long loose hair and arrays herself in her finery for the specific purpose of providing Leigh with a tantalizing display of her beauty; the description of her preparations is both provocative and sensuous. Her responses to Guy, in contrast, appear rather sterile.

For Barrett Browning, to deny a woman the right to share her husband's life, to prevent that necessary "fulness of sympathy," is basically to deny her the right to love. "A Valediction," which presents the farewell speech of a woman to a husband about to embark upon a dangerous journey, forms an appropriate lyrical companion piece to the early medieval ballads, and questions the extent to which the contemporary sentimental views of woman's role—which reflect chivalric conventions—provide women with the opportunity to love.

In "A Valediction," Barrett Browning uses the conventional situation of the valediction poem as a metaphor for the predicament of the woman who is stuck in what Ruskin later called the "place of Peace"[16] while her husband copes with the confusing and seductive dangers of the world alone. There is certainly no question of her following; she must exert what influence she can from the home. And Barrett Browning is not about to be soothed and placated with any vague reference to some undefined moral influence; she wants to know what practical help woman can provide. "Can I teach thee, my belovèd,—can I teach thee?" the speaker first asks (2.279). With her limited knowledge of the world, she recognizes, she can teach nothing of practical value. "If I said, 'Go left or right,' / The counsel would be light, / The wisdom, poor of all that could enrich thee" (2.279). "Can I bless thee" (2.279), she then asks, and realizes that the few blessings woman can provide in the home are likely to hinder, rather than help, his progress in the outside world. If she cannot follow, teach, or bless him, she concludes, she can only love him. Even this love, however, ultimately comes into question. Love involves mutual help, a sharing of life and experience; if she can do nothing for him, she cannot love him: "is *this* like love," she asks hopelessly, "to stand / With no help in my hand" (2.280). The abstract idea of love can in itself do nothing:

> Mine oath of love can swear thee
> From no ill that comes near thee,
> And thou diest while I breathe it,
> And I—I can but die!
> May GOD love thee, my belovèd,—may GOD love thee!

(2.280)

"A Valediction" provides a succinct expression of woman's frustration over her helplessness, her inability to love in the social role she is assigned.

When women are denied the right to assume any active role in a relationship, they cannot love, they can only be the passive recipients of love. While those who rebel against such limitations certainly encounter a disheartening amount of resistance, at least their awareness of the deficiencies of the role provides them with the opportunity to strive for something better. As Barrett Browning shows in "The Romance of the Swan's Nest," the situation of the woman who blindly believes in the ideals of chivalric romance, and is quite content to be loved rather than to love, is, by comparison, hopeless. In this poem, since she is attempting to show how women can be denied fulfillment in a relationship by the social and cultural notions about the feminine role which they have internalized, Barrett Browning moves away from the ballad's emphasis on story and action and begins to approach the form of the dramatic monologue. Framed by a brief introduction and conclusion, the main section of the poem focuses on the mind of a young girl, Little Ellie, as she daydreams about her future.

The sensuality in the opening description of Ellie subtly prepares the reader for the main thrust of her fantasy. Sitting on the bank of a shallow stream, Ellie luxuriates in the pleasure of holding her naked feet, "all sleek and dripping'" (3.141), in her hands while, rocking to and fro, she smiles and chooses the "sweetest pleasure" for her future (3.141). Ellie's erotic satisfaction, as her subsequent elaboration of this daydream confirms, results from envisioning herself as the object of ardent admiration and passionate desire. While the other heroines rage in frustration against the restrictions which prevent them from loving, from taking an active role in a relationship, Ellie is smugly content to derive her sensuous pleasure from being the beloved. She does not plan to love, but to "have a lover" who "shall love me without guile" (3.142), and when this lover proves himself worthy, she will give—not her love—but "Pardon / If he comes to *take* my love" (3.144; emphasis added).

Ellie, who is notably the least mature of the early heroines, has naively accepted what chivalric romance encourages women to believe. The other heroines may recognize that the "elevated" position of the traditional beloved leaves them passive and impotent, and essentially strips them of the right to love, but Ellie is quite happy as the passive beloved; she is convinced that such a position invests women with a highly desirable power. Her "power," however, lies only in her ability to decide when to relent and show mercy to her lover. While he loves "without guile" she will exert power through manipulation, by withholding her favors and forcing him to suffer and prove himself before she accepts him. A large part of her fulfillment is dependent upon denying his. The greater and more powerful the man, the greater and more powerful Ellie will feel in controlling him. Consequently, she envisions him as a duke's eldest son with a thousand serfs, a brave knight who is loved and feared by the world. Even the red-roan steed (standard accessory for the knight of romance) on which he rides will reflect his glory:

> And the steed it shall be shod
>   All in silver, housed in azure,
>   And the mane shall swim the wind;
> And the hoofs along the sod
>   Shall flash onward and keep measure,
>   Till the shepherds look behind.
>
> (3.142)

The magnificent freedom and energy represented by the horse will be harnessed by Ellie; her lover will not care for any of this glory when he gazes in her face; enslaved, he will confess: "O Love, thine eyes / Build the shrine my soul abides in, / And I kneel here for thy grace!" (3.142).

Ellie's fantasy significantly ends at the altar; she makes no attempt to consider the type of relationship which would result from this romantic court-ship. She intends, however, when they are "soul-tied by one troth" (3.144), to show him the one treasure that she possesses: a swan's nest among the reeds. Ellie dons her bonnet and goes to look at this treasure as she does every day. To her sorrow, she finds that while she has been daydreaming, "the wild swan had deserted, / And a rat had gnawed the reeds" (3.145). "Ellie went home sad and slow," the narrator concludes:

> If she found the lover ever,
>   With his red-roan steed of steeds,
> Sooth I know not; but I know
>   She could never show him—never,
>   That swan's nest among the reeds!
>
> (3.145)

The point is not that Ellie learns a lesson; it is still possible that she will find such a lover; what is important is that as long as she yearns after the chivalric ideal of love, she will never have the type of fruitful relationship that is represented by the swan's nest. The relationship of which she dreams is based only on the manipulation of power; when Ellie relents and accepts a lover, she will be left with nothing. As "The Romance of the Swan's Nest" clearly shows, chivalric ideals interfere with attainment of a happy and satisfying love not only when they lead to frustration of women's desire for something better, but also when women are persuaded that they hold the key to happiness.

By simultaneously representing and subverting cultural conventions concerning women's role in love throughout these early ballads and lyrics, Barrett Browning both reveals the shortcomings in traditional relationships and takes the first step towards defining an alternate type of relationship, a relationship which preserves women's autonomy, provides women with the opportunity to assume an active role, and consequently allows for the development of a complete "fulness of sympathy, and a sharing of life, one with another."

The Voice of Desire

As she soon demonstrates in such works as "Lady Geraldine's Courtship" and *Sonnets from the Portuguese*, Barrett Browning is quite capable of exploiting love's traditional language and imagery to suggest great passion. In "The Romance of the Swan's Nest" such language and imagery appear notably stilted and hollow, but, in this context, the resulting air of affectation is quite appropriate. For all Ellie's talk of souls, it is the forms, not the feelings behind the forms, with which she is concerned; there is no true expression of passion or desire in the poem.

Passion and desire, indeed, are seldom overtly presented in any of Barrett Browning's early poems. This is partly the result of her preference for narrative over lyric, and partly the result of her tendency to delineate the end rather than the beginning of relationships. It also, however, has much to do with the lack of an established female poetic tradition.

Barrett Browning was demonstrably familiar with the traditional romantic lyric and aware of its limitations for a woman poet. She produced a variety of translations from Petrarch's *Canzoniere*, one from Zappi's *Rime*, and was well acquainted with the works of Camoens. It may seem, indeed, rather surprising that she never published her translations of Petrarch; as Phillip Sharp has recently shown, they are quite carefully finished works. Sharp hypothesizes that since these poems were titled, polished, and transcribed in a notebook entitled *Sonnets*, Barrett Browning "may well have entertained plans of producing a selected edition of Petrarch's *Canzoniere* herself."[17] If Sharp is right, the abandoning of such a project might indicate Barrett Browning's gradual recognition of the meaninglessness of the traditional form for a woman poet.

"The Exile's Return" and "Catarina to Camoens" provide examples of Barrett Browning's original attempts to deal with this traditional form. Appropriating the two stances available to her, Barrett Browning first mimics, then revises. Both poems appear to have been prompted by the story of the Portuguese poet Camoens, and they could conceivably have originally been intended as companion pieces. According to Viscount Strangford, with whose loose translations and romanticized biography of Camoens Barrett Browning was familiar, Camoens served Catarina de Ataide, one of the queen's ladies, for many months. Eventually she was softened by his devotion and sent him a silken fillet from her hair. Camoens rushed to see her, violated the sanctity of the court, and was consequently exiled; just before he left, Catarina declared her love. When Camoens eventually won the right to return home, he discovered that she had died during his absence.[18]

Although the speaker in "The Exile's Return" is not explicitly identified as Camoens, this lyrical monologue, which records the thoughts of an exile returning home to find his beloved dead, is surely prompted by that poet's misfortunes. The poem is connected to "Catarina to Camoens" not only thematically, but also formally; the earliest extant manuscript of "Catarina to Camoens"—a text dated 1838—is, unlike the subsequent versions, stylistically highly similar to the 1838 published text of "The Exile's Return."[19]

"The Exile's Return" is one of Barrett Browning's few attempts to assume the male lyrical voice of desire, and it is not a success. The result is a dull minor poem which treats a relatively standard subject in a relatively standard manner and fails to capture any sense of passion. A grieving lover on earth addresses an ethereal beloved in heaven and draws upon the outworn set of dualities that usually accompany this subject: body and soul, turmoil and repose, anguish and tranquility, motion and fixity. The only interesting aspect of the poem is the lover's preoccupation with the devastation of death. Death parts the lovers far more completely than his exile ever could, he recognizes, and the poem repeatedly returns to his horrified apprehension of change. The physical and spiritual changes of his beloved are almost too much for him to bear, but he cannot help insistently dwelling on the strange new chill in her heart and the decay and corruption of her flesh.

While the lover is overwhelmed by the changes resulting from death in "The Exile's Return," the beloved on the verge of death in "Catarina to Camoens" desperately searches for a constant in the midst of terrifying change. Marianne Shapiro has noted that in the few cansos written by the Provençal Trobairitz or women troubadours, the "capsized" situation leads to desire expressing itself as "the wish to *be* possessed; the beloved is . . . he whom I most desire to have me."[20] The ostensibly desiring subject, therefore, is still actually the desired object. This is exactly the type of relationship that Barrett Browning rejects in "The Romance of the Swan's Nest," and yet this is all she achieves when she attempts to speak from the position of the traditionally silent beloved in "Catarina to Camoens." Although Catarina speaks, she speaks not as an active lover but as the object of Camoens' desire and, as the refrain "Sweetest eyes were ever seen" relentlessly reminds us, as the object of both his vision and his song.

The desire expressed by Catarina in this monologue, spoken while she is on her deathbed and her lover absent, is no more than the desire to remain this object, the "sweetest eyes were ever seen." Initially, she is concerned with how Camoens would react to the present changes in her eyes:

> If you stood there, would you whisper
> "Love, I love you," as before,—
> Death pervading
> Now, and shading
> Eyes you sang of, that yestreen,
> As the sweetest ever seen?

(3.124–25)

The answer to the question provides some comfort. Not only would he still call her eyes the sweetest for love's sake, but also, she thinks,

> If *you* looked down upon them,
> And if *they* looked up to *you*,
> All the light which has foregone them
> Would be gathered back anew.
> They would truly
> Be as duly
> Love-transformed to beauty's sheen,
> "Sweetest eyes were ever seen."

(3.125)

Even after death she will remain faithful, and the "sweetest eyes" will continue to watch him from heaven. But he, she suddenly realizes, may find a new beloved, and *her* eyes may become the sweetest. Since any selfish desire on Catarina's part for Camoens to continue to prefer her, rather than find happiness with another, would detract from her "sweetness," Catarina paradoxically concludes that to remain that object of love, the "sweetest eyes were ever seen," she must actually relinquish the position:

> I will look out to his future;
> I will bless it till it shine.

Should he ever be a suitor
Unto sweeter eyes than mine,
Sunshine gild them,
Angels shield them,
Whatsoever eyes terrene
Be the sweetest HIS have seen!

(3.129)

Catarina's own love, her own desire, can eventually only be expressed by the renunciation of desire.

Although "Catarina to Camoens" was an astounding success, Barrett Browning did not attempt the traditional lyric of romantic desire again—either as lover or beloved—until she had reworked the form to accommodate the forceful expression of woman's passion in *Sonnets from the Portuguese*. She did, however, like many of her contemporaries, continue to explore the question of erotic renunciation or deprivation, and the most notable expressions of female desire in her early works can actually be found in those poems in which desire is frustrated.

The women poets of the early nineteenth century may not have had an established female tradition from which to work, but there were a number of female literary roles established by the male tradition which they could appropriate, and one of the roles they adopted most frequently was the woman betrayed by a faithless lover.

A familiar figure in classical myth, the forsaken woman first becomes an important part of literary tradition with Vergil's *Aeneid* and Ovid's *Heroides*. Dido and Ariadne are particularly important characters and have a marked influence on the manner in which the forsaken woman is later depicted. These two women, I believe, become the prototypes for the two parts of a dichotomous figure: Ariadne, beating her breasts, tearing her hair, weeping, pining, and passively waiting to be consoled, becomes the sentimental deserted maiden; while Dido, full of anger and frustrated desire, violent, intense, sensual, and prepared to die, becomes the passionate abandoned woman—the woman abandoned not only *by* a lover, but also *to* her emotions. The classical influence of Ovid and Vergil can be traced throughout the following centuries as the lament of the forsaken woman is developed by such subsequent authors as Chaucer, Shakespeare, Wither, Marvell, and Pope.

It is in the nineteenth century, however, that the figure most completely captures both the popular and artistic imagination. Poe may have considered the death of a beautiful woman to be "unquestionably the most poetical topic in the world,"[21] but many Victorians would have argued that the betrayal of a beautiful woman ran a very close second. The widespread appeal of such figures as Mariana, Corinne, Oenone, and Ariadne, and of such paintings as Millais's *The Wedding Card—Jilted* and Calderon's *Broken Vows* clearly testifies to the strong interest aroused by the figure of the forsaken woman. At this time, however, the figure frequently becomes not so much an example of passionate and enduring love as an embodiment of destroyed hope. There was a notable preference for focusing on the quiet nobility of her suffering and the pathetic or morbid aspects of her predicament instead of the vigorous and passionate intensity of her desire. Although this led to the production of such fine pieces as Tennyson's "Mariana" (which does not, significantly, focus on the love story), in many minor poets it also resulted in a passionate and vital woman becoming simply pale and interesting. The abandoned woman dwindled into the pining deserted maiden, and forceful Didos gave way to sentimental Ariadnes—Ariadnes who no longer even had the energy to beat their breasts or tear their hair. The pining woman who quietly weeps, who forgives and even continues to love an unfaithful man, became a popular sentimental figure, and much maudlin verse, full of pathos and resignation, neatly turned her into love's martyr.

Dinah Mulock, for example, reverently quotes Patmore's "The Wife's Tragedy" as the epigraph to her poem "Only a Woman":

> She loves with love that cannot tire
> And if, ah, woe! she loves alone,
> Through passionate duty love flames higher,
> As grass grows taller round a stone.[22]

Following these inspirational lines, Mulock launches into a highly emotional monologue in which a wife comes to terms with her husband's philandering and eventually finds consolation in her own constancy and the slight possibility that perhaps, "As the solemn years go by, / He will think sometimes with regretful sigh, / The other woman was less true than I."[23] Caroline Norton, who had more than enough reason to be bitter, nevertheless displays such immense magnanimity in her description of ideal "Woman's Love" that her sincerity must surely be suspect:

> To keep unchanged thy calm, pure, quiet love,
> If he, inconstant, doth a new one prove:
> To love all round as a part of him,
> Ev'n her he worships:—though thine eye be dim
> With weeping for thyself: to pray that not
> One cloud may darken o'er *their* earthly lot;
> With the affection of true hearts, to see
> His happiness, which doth not hang on thee;—
> Oh! this is woman's love—its joy—its pain;
> And this—it hath been felt—and felt in vain.[24]

Letitia Landon, in her most characteristic manner, turns the same sentiment into pure doggerel:

> Lovely as the flowers below,
>   Changeless as the stars on high.
> Made all chance and change to prove,
>   And this is a woman's love.[25]

Man's infidelity is reduced to little more than a test by which the true nature of woman's love can be revealed in all its glory.

While these minor women poets tended only to echo the common sentimental perspective, more accomplished women gradually learned to adapt the poetry of loss, suffering, and endurance to accommodate and reveal the female lyric voice of desire. The frustration of love in their poems imposes distance, and distance serves the same function here as in the traditional male lyric—it maintains the sharp edge of desire. By suggesting the hidden erotic passion that continues to rage beneath the surface of passive acceptance, or more directly by resurrecting Dido and discarding Ariadne, these women transformed the lyrical complaint of suffering and endurance into the female equivalent of the masculine lyric of distance and desire; the aesthetic of renunciation was gradually discarded, and the woman abandoned to emotion assumed a central role in their poetry.

In the first of her poems to focus on a forsaken woman, Barrett Browning does not actually adapt the prevalent type of the deserted maiden so much as simply reject it. She makes a particular point of undermining the potential sweet pathos of the situation, and her strong and angry heroine certainly does not fit the conventional noble mold. Barrett Browning's tale of betrayal, "A Romance of the Ganges," was written specifically for *Findens' Tableaux* at Mary Russell Mitford's request. "I want you to write me a poem," Mitford wrote,

> in illustration of a very charming group of Hindoo girls floating their lamps upon the Ganges—launching them, I should say. You know that pretty superstition [if the girl's lamp fails, her lover is inconstant]. . . . I could not think of going to press without your assistance, and have chosen for you the very prettiest subject and, I think, the prettiest plate of the whole twelve.[26]

Everything about this illustration is indeed "charming" and "pretty." In the foreground, the light falls upon a doll-like figure who, unlike the other women depicted, has strictly Caucasian features. This sweet and beautiful young girl is daintily and confidently launching her lamp. Behind her in the shadows, an older, darker, and rather nondescript woman leans hopelessly against a tree, her body slumped and her eyes downcast.[27] All the ingredients for creating a poem of great pathos are present, but if Mitford expected a "charming" and "pretty" tale to accompany the engraving, she must have been disappointed.

To begin with, while Mitford finds the superstition quaint and pretty, Barrett Browning seems to find it faintly ridiculous:

> Why, all the stars are ready
>   To symbolize the soul,
> The stars untroubled by the wind,
>   Unwearied as they roll;
> And yet the soul by instinct sad
>   Reverts to symbols low—
> To that small flame, whose very name
>   Breathed o'er it, shakes it so!
>
> (2.30)

In the opening stanza, Barrett Browning begins by duplicating the calm, trance-like aura of the scene depicted; the earth sleeps quietly, and the soothing voice of the river seems the "voice of dreams" (2.29). This drowsy peace does not last long; the maidens bring onto the scene the "human heart wherein / No nightly calm can be" (2.29), and Barrett Browning reveals that chaos, anger and violence have been seething beneath the superficial calm. The main character in the poem is Luti. She is, as Dorothy Mermin notes, "a powerful and self-assertive woman, but in Barrett Browning's ballads men generally prefer weak ones."[28] Luti's strength and assertiveness do not serve her well in love; she is discarded for a pliable woman with more conventional appeal. The light in her boat soon fails, but Luti refuses to weep for the lover whose faithlessness she has long suspected. Instead, she calls upon Nuleeni to launch her boat. Nuleeni is youthful, shy, and meek—obviously the doll-like figure in the foreground of the illustration—and she is also, as Luti has guessed, the new object of the false lover's affections. Her light lasts. The betrayed Luti is no doubt intended to correspond to the sorrowful maiden slumped against the tree, but Barrett Browning is not about to have her heroine pine away in heroic unhappiness—Luti gets revenge. With a dread laugh and wild dilated eyes, she ensures that the innocent Nuleeni is well aware that the lover previously belonged to her and is clearly therefore untrustworthy—no matter what the light might indicate. Then she jumps in the river. Nuleeni's light may endure, but her happiness is nevertheless spoiled by the revelations and the suicide of the betrayed woman:

> Frail symbols? None are frail enow
>   For mortal joys to borrow!—
> While bright doth float Nuleeni's boat,
>   She weepeth dark with sorrow.
>
> (2.37)

Luti's frustrated desires emerge in anger and violence, and she consequently displays a vindictiveness that is essentially at odds with Barrett Browning's conception of love; none of her later heroines is ever allowed to exact such tragic vengeance—at least intentionally. Nor, however, do they simply lapse into the role of the conventional lovelorn maiden, suffering in heroic silence. Barrett Browning has little patience with this angelic ideal and strong doubts concerning the possibility of her existence.

The rejected woman in Barrett Browning's poems usually continues to love, but repressed desire inevitably emerges in various contradictory ways. Continuing love causes the woman to desire her beloved's continuing happiness, and so she attempts to endure suffering and to forgive him. That same love, however, leads her to continue to desire him for herself, and this desire expresses itself in bitterness, resentment, and self-pity. In two minor dramatic monologues, "That Day" and "Change upon Change," Barrett Browning experiments with delving into the mind of an abandoned woman in order to capture the tension which would inevitably result from these conflicting emotions. The scene set in each poem is basically the same: the rejected woman returns to the place by the river where her lover first vowed to be true. The lonely brooding speaker in "That Day" claims to forgive him for being unfaithful and hopes he will remain calm and untroubled; he remains her beloved even if he has not been her lover since that day. Protestations of love and forgiveness, however, are sporadically interrupted by outbreaks of bitterness—the man is a "vow-breaker" guilty of "treason" (3.107)—and the woman's attempt to exercise restraint and control is undercut by her morbid tendency to dwell on frustration, isolation, and despondency.

In "Change upon Change," the bitterness is even stronger. Remembering her false lover's vows of endless devotion, this woman attempts to justify his inexcusable behavior in an argument which gradually grows sharply ironic. First, she contrasts the present scene with the former; summer has given way to winter, the flowers are now withered, and the stream frozen and mute. In the natural changes of the landscape she attempts to find justification for her lover's freedom to change, to "love and go"; "why," she asks, "since these be changed since May, / Should *thou* change less than *they?*" (3.211). The false lightness of her tone clearly suggests her awareness of the speciousness of her argument, and the jump in her logic becomes particularly notable when she next begins to justify her own change. She has grown tearful and as pale as the snow which covers the earth. This change, however, is not natural; it is the direct result of his faithlessness, and, as the repetition, meter, and rhyme reflect growing distress, she concludes by relinquishing the false argument:

> If my face is turned too pale,
> It was thine oath that first did fail,—

> It was thy love proved false and frail,—
> And why, since these be changed enow,
> Should *I* change less than *thou?*

> (3.211)

The theme of frustrated love and continuing desire is most skillfully dealt with in one of the most important of the 1844 poems, the dramatic monologue "Bertha in the Lane."[29] This poem records the death-bed speech of a woman who has learned that her fiancé, Robert, loves her younger sister, Bertha. Keeping her discovery a secret, she has resolved to renounce all claim to Robert for her sister's sake and has sewn a shroud and a wedding gown. As the poem opens, she presents this gown to the understandably startled Bertha and retires to bed. She then reveals to her sister how she overheard Robert declaring his love to Bertha in the lane on the spring day when they went gathering May bloom for the bees. She repeatedly declares her continuing love for Bertha, attempts to justify and forgive the treacherous Robert, and finally, calling upon Christ, she dies.

The basic story of the two sisters is relatively common and has been given a wide variety of endings. In the ballad "The Twa Sisters," the eldest girl is so envious of her fair sister that "Wi'grief an' spite she almost brast."[30] Instead of passively relinquishing her lover, she drowns the younger girl. Hidden desire emerges with violent results. Letty Landon's "The Secret Discovered," in contrast, has a heroine of unbelievable goodness.[31] She puts aside her own love without a word of protest, only wanting her sister and her lover to be happy, and dedicates the remainder of her life to taking care of her father. Hidden desire remains totally repressed, and Landon's heroine becomes the perfect example of womanly self-sacrifice.

Barrett Browning's contemporaries generally viewed Bertha's elder sister in much the same way. Although all the romantic ballads were received with delight, "Bertha in the Lane" was frequently singled out for particular praise. *Blackwood's* found it "the gem" of the 1844 collection, and the "purest picture of a broken heart that ever drew tears from the eyes of woman or of man."[32] The poem soon became renowned for the prodigious quantity of tears it inspired—and the high quality; Barrett Browning recorded with ironic delight the endless gush reputed to have flowed down the "Plutonian cheeks of a lawyer unknown" (EBB 1.247).

While the poem was unanimously acclaimed for its pathetic beauty and womanly tenderness, the presentation of the dying girl caused an interesting twinge of uneasiness in two particular reviewers. Chorley, in the *Athenaeum*, thought the poem had one "defect": the "disclosure which the heroic sister makes of her own sacrifice."[33] Instead of dying quietly, this disappointed lady makes sure her sister is fully aware of the sacrifices made for her sake—and this troubled Chorley. The *Westminster Review*, convinced the speaker's words were her dying benediction upon Bertha, was similarly disturbed by her repeatedly expressed desire to keep the betrothal ring, even in the grave. Her request was surely, he assumed, "a cruel coincidence." Inadvertently putting his finger on the crux of the poem, he concluded in confusion, "Her blessings meant for dew congeal like icicles."[34] To account for their uneasy sense that certain aspects of the poem were at odds with its apparent celebration of woman's altruistic love, both reviewers decided that the poem must be flawed, that Barrett Browning had lost control over her art. The possibility that these "flaws" might be an integral part of the poem was never considered.

Modern critics, having little taste for treachery, jilts, and broken hearts, have generally ignored "Bertha in the Lane," and the speaker has been dismissed as a "dying angel,"[35] one of those provoking figures of tearful nobility and immense sensibility which are liberally scattered throughout conduct books and keepsake annuals. But "Bertha in the Lane" is far more than a simple sentimental ballad, and the speaker is no keepsake maiden. The Victorians' admiration for the poem—and the modern critics' distaste—is based only on a reading of the surface text; Barrett Browning's concern in this poem is with repressed desires, the possible layers of truth which lie beneath surfaces. While the surface text may seem to glorify the dying sister's sacrifice, the sub-text reveals the persistence of passion, a strong undercurrent of resentment, and a deep-rooted unwillingness to assume the disagreeable role of martyr.

The speaker, whom I shall call elder sister, had been charged with the care of Bertha when her mother died. Now, having fulfilled her responsibilities and sacrificed her own happiness for the younger girl's sake, she calls upon the dead mother to witness that she is giving all the "gifts required" (3.98): hope, happiness, love, and soon, even life itself. Shrined in "molten glory" (3.98), the mother's ghost appears, the embodiment of the saintly ideal of womanly duty.[36] She is a cold, hard, and comfortless ideal. Her smile, "bright and bleak," is like "cold waves" (3.98) washing over the desire of elder sister. She drains her daughter of all strength, leaves her sobbing weakly, and, most importantly, begins to deprive her of the power of speech. The mother encourages the girl to act in the manner most likely to guarantee Bertha's happiness, to repress her own desires and die in heroic silence. Elder sister is not quite ready for that. Her mother's chilly brightness is still being challenged by the warm and irresistible light of earthly love. "Ghostly mother," she says,

> keep aloof
> One hour longer from my soul,
> For I still am thinking of
> Earth's warm-beating joy and dole!
> On my finger is a ring

> Which I still see glittering
> When the night hides everything.
>
> (3.99)

As the reference to the ring reveals, although she has decided to renounce all claim to Robert, she continues to love him and cannot help harboring a desperate hope that he will return, shamefaced and repentant. She continually fancies that she hears someone arriving. "No one standeth in the street?" (3.98) she first asks Bertha somewhat casually. Then, more urgently, "Hush!—look out— / Up the street! Is none without?" (3.102). And finally:

> Are there footsteps at the door?
> Look out quickly. Yea, or nay?
> Someone might be waiting for
> Some last word that I might say.
>
> (3.104)

When her last hope of seeing Robert again is gone, she takes some consolation in imagining that he will arrive after her death. Carefully, she plans the stage for this final reunion. "When I wear the shroud I made," she tells Bertha,

> Let the folds lie straight and neat,
> And the rosemary be spread,
> That if any friend should come,
> (To see *thee*, Sweet!) all the room
> May be lifted out of gloom.
>
> And, dear Bertha, let me keep
> On my hand this little ring.
>
> (3.105)

That ring, emblem of Robert's now forgotten desire for her, elder sister cannot renounce; she must take it with her to the grave. The presence of the ring and the rosemary—emblem of remembrance and frequently used at weddings to signify fidelity in love—seems to suggest that in preparation for this grave, elder sister is arranging herself as a bride awaiting her groom.[37] This pathetic attempt to cling to a few last remnants of human affection is rather moving and certainly understandable, but since she plans this charming scene entirely for Robert's benefit, the probable effects on him should not be ignored. Her carefully planned tableau might then suggest a desire to make her treacherous lover suffer appropriately. It will surely guarantee that he never forgets he is, as Robert Browning noted, a real "ladykiller" (RB 2.1043). The ambiguity of the scene aptly reflects the rejected woman's conflicting emotions.

Elder sister's relationship with Bertha reveals a similarly troubling ambiguity. If she desired only to be the martyr, only to make Bertha happy, the most charitable thing would be to do as the dead mother urges, to say nothing at all—or Barrett Browning could have written the monologue without an auditor. Bertha's presence suggests there must be some reason for the revelations. This is not just the incoherent rambling of a feverish dying woman. Her disclosure is quite deliberately made—and introduced with an appropriately dramatic flourish. "Lean down closer," she demands of Bertha, "closer still! / I have words thine ear to fill, / And would kiss thee at my will" (3.99). This rather unsettling insistence on closeness is found throughout the opening stanzas and points to one possible explanation for the disclosure.

As substitute mother, elder sister has made all the sacrifices demanded; she believes that she has loved Bertha with a "love complete" (3.97). But to be expected to give all and demand nothing in return is surely pressing the limits of human generosity. The girl understandably wants to know that her sacrifice is appreciated and her love returned. Considering the situation, it is not surprising that she should have some doubts about Bertha. We are not told exactly what Bertha was up to in that lane. When Robert declared that he loved her and only *"esteemed"* elder sister (3.103), Bertha made "Good true answers" for her sister's sake, but it does not necessarily follow that she rejected Robert. And the relationship has obviously progressed since then. Bertha certainly makes no attempt to decline the offer of either gown or groom, and as she squirms, blushes, and avoids her sister's eyes, her absolute innocence becomes somewhat questionable. Repeatedly, therefore, elder sister seeks confirmation of their continuing love and intimacy. "Lean thy face down," she tells Bertha,

> drop it in
> These two hands, that I may hold
> 'Twixt their palms thy cheek and chin,
> Stroking back the curls of gold:
> 'Tis a fair, fair face, in sooth.
>
> (3.97)

There is something vaguely disturbing about this passage. Elder sister becomes reminiscent of Salome or Judith—not because she gets Bertha's pretty white neck conveniently close, but because her demonstration of affection becomes uncomfortably similar to an assertion of power. She is forcing the frightened girl to submit to her caresses. Bertha apparently shrinks away, and elder sister, sadly saying "Dost thou mind me, Dear, so much," seeks verbal confirmation of love instead. "Have I not been nigh a mother" she asks, and "Have we not loved one another" (3.98). Bertha remains provokingly silent.

Providing Bertha with a detailed analysis of her sufferings, therefore, seems to be elder sister's final attempt to extract some proof of gratitude and affection;

unable to bury her own desires completely, she continues to crave love from both Robert and Bertha. This makes her a more sympathetic figure than she would be if she were intentionally seeking some subtle revenge, and we could hear the malicious cackle behind the words. But it makes little difference to the effects on Bertha. Elder sister relies on the potential powers of the victim, the tactics of the martyr wishing to inspire guilt. Although we never actually hear her say "After all I've done for you . . ." the point is well made. The reader's response to elder sister is consequently ambivalent. Her self-sacrifice may be admirable. Her need for proof of affection and gratitude is understandable. But she extracts a terrible price for her own suffering and loss: her heroic love feeds on Bertha's guilt and ultimately leaves the younger girl with little chance for future happiness with Robert. The vengeful Luti could do no better.

Elder sister's desire to ingratiate herself with Bertha—not to antagonize her—seems to be confirmed by her refusal to speculate about Bertha's possible role in the affair. Throughout the poem, she concentrates on excusing Robert. "Could he help it, if my hand / He had claimed with hasty claim?" she asks (3.101). The answer indisputably being yes, she falls back on a useful old line: "That was wrong perhaps—but then / Such things be—and will again. / Women cannot judge for men" (3.101). She pathetically clings to the comforting notion that Bertha is an ally, not a rival. She sees Bertha and herself forming a cosy confederation of women, linked by their common inability to understand man. "Could we blame him," she concludes in resignation, "Thou and I, Dear, if we might?" (3.101). Man's well-known weakness for plump rosy cheeks and golden curls makes Robert's preference for Bertha inevitable, she decides. While Bertha is the perfect rose, she is only the pale crocus growing close by, necessarily trodden underfoot as Robert eagerly scrambles for the tantalizing superior blossom. Or, she is like the May bloom and Bertha the merry summer bee. "Fit," she resolves with forced gaiety, "that I be plucked for thee!" (3.104).

The rose may be the choice bloom, but elder sister's crocus and May are emblems of young love and marriage, and it is, after all, her hopes of these that have been so cruelly trampled. Self-pity lurks close to the surface of these futile attempts at justification, and it is not surprising that Bertha repeatedly breaks down shaking and weeping. After each outburst of tears, elder sister hastens to comfort Bertha and disclaim any feelings of resentment, but her anxious efforts are in vain. "Do not weep so—Dear,—heart-warm," she insists:

> All was best as it befell.
> If I say he did me harm,
>   I speak wild,—I am not well.
> All his words were kind and good—
> *He esteemed me!*

(3.103)

The emphasis supplied by the italics, showing how his cold esteem rankles, clearly belies her assertion that his words were kind and good. Underlying bitterness and persistent desire continually emerge to shatter the veneer of calm acceptance.

The bitterness and self-pity are most striking when elder sister specifically recalls the events of that day when they went gathering May bloom for the bees. Since she is attempting to appeal to Bertha's emotions, she does not just recount what she heard of Bertha and Robert's clandestine conversation; this is only vaguely suggested. Instead, she provides a moving description of how she felt before and after. As she relives the experience, she simply cannot avoid appearing resentful, and the implications of the story gradually undermine the accompanying words of comfort and justification.

Elder sister begins by remembering the intense pleasure and peacefulness she initially experienced:

> What a day it was, that day!
>   Hills and vales did openly
> Seem to heave and throb away
>   At the sight of the great sky:
> And the silence, as it stood
> In the glory's golden flood,
> Audibly did bud, and bud.

                                                                    (3.99–100)

The fecundity and sexual suggestiveness of this passage aptly reflect elder sister's growing joy as she awaited her marriage to Robert. Her desire for erotic satisfaction, now frustrated, is displaced into an almost voluptuous landscape. Full of youth and promise, she was like a flower on the point of bursting into bloom, and as she smiled over the May blossoms that she had gathered, she thought lovingly of Bertha and knew perfect happiness in this earthly paradise. Bertha, crying bitterly on hearing this, clearly feels like the snake.

An entirely different landscape faced elder sister after overhearing Robert's declaration of love to Bertha. When she awoke from a long swoon, it was night, and she was "cold and stark" (3.102). Her previous joyful communion with nature was replaced by a frightening sense of alienation. The moon, the stars, and the May blooms, she recalls, "seemed to wonder what I was" (3.102). Self-pity and resentment become quite clear as, for the first time, she explicitly links her approaching death to the loss of Robert. "I answered coldly," she reminds Bertha,

> When you met me at the door;
> And I only *heard* the dew
> Dripping from me to the floor:

And the flowers, I bade you see,
Were too withered for the bee,—
As my life, henceforth, for me.

(3.103)

Barrett Browning is frequently accused of unnecessarily indulging in the senti-mental, but as this passage shows, she often does this for a specific effect; elder sister, as she wallows in self-pity, always seems to have one eye on Bertha, carefully gauging the responses to each pathetic pronouncement.

No matter how often elder sister professes love for Bertha and forgiveness for Robert, her story firmly establishes their responsibility for her transformation from promising bud to withered bloom. She may be entirely sincere when she concludes her account of that day by telling Bertha "Sweet, be merry!" (3.104), but there is little chance of Bertha ever being "merry" after this. The dying girl's bid for affection is a resounding success. Once again she demands proof of love: "Art thou near me?" she calls out, "nearer! so—" (3.105). Obviously feeling the full weight of a guilty conscience, Bertha is now crushed and pliant and silently obeys. Elder sister is satisfied with this proof of love, and, "death-strong" (3.106), she completes the sacrifice; Bertha, meekly fulfilling one last request, is left easing the life out of the dying girl with her kisses.

"Bertha in the Lane" cannot be dismissed as just a simple romantic ballad, and it is not surprising that those two early reviewers registered some uneasiness with the poem. Barrett Browning has a highly sophisticated awareness of the intricacies of love and sacrifice, and the dramatic monologue provides her with an effective means of revealing the persistent desire of an apparently dutiful and loving girl. Elder sister is incapable of truly becoming a "dying angel." Her love is strong and enduring, but still marked by a very human selfishness. As Gilbert and Gubar rightly observe, to be completely selfless is "not only to be noble, it is to be dead";[38] elder sister cannot relinquish all desire until she is dead. Her resentment and unwillingness to assume the role of martyr are never overcome, and her continuing desire for affection leads her to spoil the sacrifice that she makes. She leaves Bertha not only Robert—a questionable prize and probably now unwanted—but also a weighty legacy of guilt. Her blessings do indeed "congeal like icicles."

In Barrett Browning's early experiments with the figure of the forsaken woman, the voice of female desire may emerge only indirectly, but it is never-theless a strong and aggressive voice; frustration of desire does not automatically lead to passive suffering and restraint in these works. The deserted maiden is gradually being transformed into the abandoned woman, and her lament adapted to give forceful expression to the female lyric voice of desire; in the later "Bianca among the Nightingales," the transformation will be complete.

The problem of woman's voice which Barrett Browning tackles in these poems is closely connected to her other major concern in the early ballads and lyrics—the problem of woman's role in romantic relationships. In the early devotional poetry, God is seen to provide His weary child, His beloved, with a longed-for release from troubling human passion; He "strikes a silence through you all" (2.87), Barrett Browning writes, and He offers a peaceful refuge from the world in sleep-like death. The desire to withdraw from the world, to sink into this perfect and placid form of ultimate passivity, is soon rejected in the romance ballads and succeeded by an even stronger desire for the satisfactions that human love can provide. Convention and tradition, however, seem to conspire to reinforce the previously renounced impulses towards child-like passivity and silence in women; women are denied both an active role in sexual relationships and an active voice in love poetry. These impulses, Barrett Browning suggests, must be resisted, and in the poems of and about love which follow the early ballads and lyrics, she continues to insist upon the necessity of releasing women from the passivity and silence imposed upon them in life and art by the role of beloved, and to attempt to provide women with both a functional role and a forceful voice.

3

Geraldine's Courtship: The Vision Speaks

Among Barrett Browning's contemporaries, one of the most popular of the early ballads and lyrics was "Lady Geraldine's Courtship."[1] The poem was warmly admired by Carlyle, Martineau, and the Rossettis, among others, and frequently singled out for particular praise by the critics. Barrett Browning, who had written the poem hastily to meet a publisher's deadline, was amused and surprised by its success and believed that it had attracted "more attention than its due" (EBB 1.211). Modern critics have wholeheartedly agreed, and done more than enough to compensate for any overindulgence on the part of nineteenth-century readers. The poem now rarely attracts critical attention, and, when it does, it is usually dismissed as no more than a particularly uninspired example of Barrett Browning's early ballad romances.[2]

But "Lady Geraldine's Courtship," the last of the 1844 poems to be written, is not actually a ballad, and has little in common with such poems as "The Romaunt of the Page" and "Rhyme of the Duchess May." Both thematically and stylistically, this poem reveals a significant advance in Barrett Browning's treatment of the subject of love. The early ballads almost consistently focus on the failure of love; the heroines are repeatedly frustrated in their attempts to establish lasting and satisfying relationships by the intervention of death, the inconstancy of their lovers, or—most importantly—the passive roles imposed upon them by conventional notions concerning the proper behavior for women in love. And even when Barrett Browning does write of a happy, although short-lived, union in "Rhyme of the Duchess May," she makes little attempt to describe the love which drives May to elope with Sir Guy. She sweeps right past the initial joys of love and fixes firmly on its eventual sorrows.

In "Lady Geraldine's Courtship," Barrett Browning is interested in bringing love to life for the reader, not in tracing the reasons for its demise; for the first time, a successful romantic relationship becomes the focus of her attention. And the relationship is shown to succeed primarily because the heroine is not confined to that restrictive position of passive and silent beloved against which Barrett Browning's earlier female characters so vainly rebelled. There is a new emphasis on the woman's potential to be the active subject in a narrative, the lover rather than merely the beloved—an emphasis which leads to a deliberate confounding of traditional lovers' roles. The title itself, "Lady Geraldine's Courtship," piquantly raises this issue in providing us with no context by which to ascertain whether this is grammatically an objective or subjective genitive: it could equally mean "The Courtship of Lady Geraldine (by Bertram)" or "Lady Geraldine's Courtship (of Bertram)." The poem at large demonstrates that the genitive leans more to the subjective than the objective and that Geraldine is the active lover. Along with this new emphasis on woman as lover rather than beloved, there is a movement away from a preoccupation with plot to a concern with relationship and a resulting interest in experimenting with sensuous language to convey the physical and the spiritual nature of the relationship; "Lady Geraldine's Courtship" consequently marks an important turning point in Barrett Browning's conception and treatment of the question of love.

The main narrator of this romantic tale is Bertram, a poor poet who is invited by the wealthy and powerful Lady Geraldine to Wycombe Hall. Lady Geraldine and Bertram spend many hours discussing such topics as the primary importance of the soul and the basic nobility of all men, and Bertram comes to believe that she is sympathetic to his radical social theories; he falls in love with her, but assumes his passion to be hopeless. One morning, he overhears Geraldine tell an overly persistent suitor, an earl, that she will marry only a wealthy and noble man. "I shall never blush," she claims, "to think how he was born" (2.299). Bertram, misunderstanding her words, angrily rushes into the room, denounces her for scorning the common man, and declares that he has dared to love her. His passionate tirade over, he hears Lady Geraldine say his name and swoons away at her feet; when he awakens in another room, he begins to write the letter to a friend which comprises the main body of the poem. In a brief conclusion, Barrett Browning adopts an omniscient narrator to describe Geraldine as she comes to Bertram's room and declares her love for him, and the poem ends with Bertram kneeling before Geraldine while she whispers triumphantly: "It shall be as I have sworn. / Very rich he is in virtues, very noble—noble, certes; / And I shall not blush in knowing that men call him lowly born" (2.310).

This "Romance of the Age," which replaces exotic landscapes and ancient days with the Victorian drawing room, may not be as colorful as "A Romance of the Ganges" or "The Romaunt of the Page," but it is psychologically far more interesting. In the early ballads, Barrett Browning generally employs an omniscient narrator, but does not often take advantage of the opportunity this provides to suggest the thoughts and feelings of her characters or to explore their emotional responses to each other; as is usual in ballads, the events of the story take precedence over the developing inner lives of the characters.[3] In "Lady Geraldine's Courtship," the inner life predominates; the poem has "more mysticism (or what is called mysticism) in it," Barrett Browning claimed, "hid in the story . . . than all the other ballad-poems of the two volumes" (MRM 3.49). This poem is actually more like a dramatic monologue than a ballad: Bertram's perceptions and in particular his responses to Geraldine, become of far greater significance than the actual events he describes.

The main narrative, the letter written by Bertram, is complicated by the presence of three different perspectives. First, there are the two perspectives provided directly by Bertram. The young man who records the events of the preceding days is painfully aware of his love for Lady Geraldine and believes that she scorns him as lowly born; his resulting bitterness and cynicism frequently emerge to color his narrative. He is trying, however, to convey not only his present unhappiness, but also his thoughts and feelings as he lived through these experiences. Consequently, as he becomes caught up in his memories, Bertram also appears as the idealistic romantic, smitten by the woman he sees as representative of "all of good and all of fair" (2.282). These two perspectives rarely emerge as distinctly as I have presented them, and, as a result, the young poet's narrative is sometimes marked by contradiction or ambivalence: descriptions of lingering tenderness can be quickly succeeded by, or mixed with, the bitter recriminations of the lover scorned.

Bertram's dual perspective, however, does not dominate the poem completely. Barrett Browning actually creates two distinct strands of narrative: Bertram's story, which is given directly, and Geraldine's, which must be deduced. As Bertram describes Lady Geraldine and recalls what she did and said, the reader pieces together a second, and more accurate, underlying narrative which tells of Geraldine's responses to, and growing love for, the young poet. Since Bertram tells the story, his narrative obviously appears to dominate the text, but Barrett Browning continually distances the reader from his perspective and encourages the construction of Geraldine's alternative narrative—a narrative which eventually defines our reading of the text. Geraldine never becomes lost as the silent passive object in Bertram's story; she is too clearly established as the active speaking subject in her own.

The clarity with which Geraldine's voice emerges becomes particularly notable if the poem is compared to Tennyson's "Locksley Hall" (1842). Barrett Browning was no doubt influenced by this recently published work when she wrote "Lady Geraldine's Courtship," and contemporary reviewers frequently classed the two works together.[4] They are similar not only in verse form (the monologue in eight-foot trochaic couplets), but also in situation (the poor lover in the aristocrat's mansion), in tone (the oscillation between extremes of love and scorn, optimism and pessimism), and in social commentary (the attack on the false values of the age). But Tennyson's Amy always remains a shadowy figure; while the rejected lover's bitter assessment of his "shallow-hearted" cousin, much like Bertram's assessment of Geraldine, tends to be undermined, we can nevertheless deduce very little about Amy's true motives and feelings. Barrett Browning provides what might be seen as a feminine response to "Locksley Hall" when she appropriates Tennyson's subject and then neatly subordinates the male voice of the actual speaker and allows the female voice, which previously remained silent, indirectly to control the reader's understanding of the text.

In attempting to distance the reader from Bertram's perspective, Barrett Browning ensures that he does not always appear as a sympathetic figure. His most objectionable feature stems, somewhat paradoxically, from his most admirable. Bertram's democratic views allow for no distinction to be made on the grounds of birth, wealth, or social position. The primary importance of the soul and the irrelevance of worldly trappings are subjects of which he never tires. They form the basis for both a scornful summary of British social law (2.289–90) and an ironic lecture on the "wondrous age" of progress which is more concerned with the development of iron than the development of the soul (2.294–95). As he indicates when, enraged, he suggests that Lady Geraldine needs to show "more reverence . . . not for rank or wealth . . . / But for Adam's seed, MAN!" (2.301–2), Bertram is convinced of the basic nobility of all men. Everyone, he grandly announces, is stamped with "God's image" and has "God's kindling breath within" (2.302).

But Bertram is an inverted snob. Although his scorn for Lady Geraldine's fashionable friends seems to be justified, he nevertheless frequently appears to have a weighty chip on his shoulder. He is much too quick to dismiss the wealthy and nobly born with disdainful generalizations. Barrett Browning's attempt to distance the reader from Bertram is perhaps overly successful when she depicts him storming into the room to denounce Geraldine. In Bertram's presence, Geraldine displays the conventional signs of love: she trembles and is alternately flushed and pale. Bertram's response is unforgivable, even if his pride has been hurt; he is far too smug: "'tis so always with a worldly man or woman / In the presence of true spirits," he sneers, "what else *can* they do but quail?" (2.300).

Understandably, the peasant poet has not proved to be one of Barrett Browning's more popular creations. Edmund Stedman, for one, found him insufferable. In "Lady Geraldine's Courtship," Stedman wrote, Barrett Browning only showed

> how meanly a womanish fellow might act. . . . [Bertram] is a dreadful prig, who cries, mouths, and faints like a schoolgirl, allowing himself to eat the bread of the Philistines and betray his sense of inequality, and upon whom Lady Geraldine certainly throws herself away.[5]

Stedman's response is extreme, however, and his understanding of the poem questionable. Barrett Browning is not interested in creating a strong and spotless white knight for Geraldine, and Bertram comes alive for the reader precisely because of his unforgettable flaws.

Barrett Browning also encourages the continual construction of Geraldine's alternative narrative by revealing Bertram to be an unreliable narrator and a poor interpreter of Lady Geraldine. Initially, he seems to attribute her flattering attentions to a taste for poetry and sympathy with his democratic views. After overhearing her conversation with the earl, he assumes that she is actually no better than her companions and has only been idly amusing herself. He was no more, he tells his friend, than a momentary diversion, a household pet like her greyhound, a dog whose antics are encouraged when it is convenient but who is scorned and sent home as soon as he becomes tiresome.

The reader is never misled by Geraldine's response to the earl. Her attraction to the poet and her scorn for society's values are immediately apparent when she singles Bertram out with an invitation to Wycombe Hall. The invitation, extended in the presence of her friends, results in a sudden telling silence. Geraldine colors, and although Bertram interprets this as a momentary blush of shame, her subsequent words indicate that it is more likely to be a flush of anger. "I am seeking," she says with cold deliberation, "more distinction than these gentlemen think worthy of my claim" (2.284); "these gentlemen" are clearly thinking nothing of the sort, and her cool polite formality only thinly veils an aggressive challenge to their arrogant pretensions.

Geraldine's attraction to Bertram becomes even clearer after his arrival at Wycombe Hall. On the very first morning of his visit, she leads him and her other guests directly to the statue of Silence in her garden. Her following commentary on the statue suggests that this scene has been carefully staged— and staged entirely for Bertram's benefit. She is eager to demonstrate that she too is unimpressed by outer show and concerned only with spiritual excellence. While the typical statue of silence has her left hand's index finger on her lips to say "Hush," Geraldine's Silence is asleep; her finger has fallen on her cheek and her symbol rose is held only slackly. This particular interpretation of the conventional form, Geraldine says, suggests how the "essential meaning growing may exceed the special symbol" (2.289). The statue may no longer display all the expected attributes of a typical figure of Silence, but it has become a truer representation of the *concept* of silence. This, she continues, "applies more high and low. / Our true noblemen will often through right nobleness grow humble, / And assert an inward honour by denying outward show" (2.289). Bertram gives Geraldine no opportunity to continue and to explain how the concept applies to the low—although he might have found this instructive. His favorite topic has just been raised, and in he jumps, determined to prove Geraldine wrong. The result is a verbal tug of war. While Geraldine is vainly struggling to convey a personal conviction to Bertram, he views the discussion purely on a general level. "Let the poets dream such dreaming!

madam, in these British islands / 'Tis the substance that wanes ever, 'tis the symbol that exceeds" (2.289). Geraldine is not about to give up and insistently returns the subject to the personal:

> Not so quickly . . . I confess, where'er you go, you
> Find for things, names—shows for actions, and pure gold for honour clear:
> But when all is run to symbol in the Social, I will throw you
> The world's book which now reads dryly, and sit down with Silence here.
>
> (2.290)

While the reader may see a subtle message of encouragement to the young poet in Geraldine's argument, Bertram misses the point entirely. He may hold democratic views in theory, but—quite understandably—the possibility that the wealthy and powerful Lady Geraldine might be romantically interested in him, a lowly born poet, never enters his mind. Before Bertram can recognize that she not only seriously accepts his democratic theories but is quite prepared to put them into practice, Geraldine must literally become the active subject in the narrative. She must take the initiative and explicitly declare her love.

As this resolution to the poem indicates, the active role of lover in "Lady Geraldine's Courtship" is not restricted to Bertram; the roles of lover and beloved are as interchangeable as the positions of narrative subject and object. This is one of the most significant ways in which "Lady Geraldine's Courtship" differs from Barrett Browning's medieval ballads—and possibly one of the reasons it is "A Romance of the Age." Although they focus primarily on the female perspective, the early ballads show the roles of men and women to be firmly, and often even fatally, fixed according to traditional standards. Barrett Browning now moves in the direction of the later poems by suggesting an interchangeability of roles in the lovers' relationship and showing a hero and heroine who are equally suited to the roles of both lover and beloved.

Initially, the reader no doubt approaches the poem with the standard expectation that Bertram will appear as the lover and Geraldine the beloved, and the opening stanzas seem to confirm such an assumption by placing Bertram in the most conventional of lover's roles: the troubadour, the poet-lover "singing" to the beautiful noble lady whom he apparently has no hope of winning. The most notable features of this traditional lover are his romantic deification of the beloved and his accompanying conviction of unworthiness. Bertram quickly demonstrates that he conforms to the type. There is an important distinction, however, between the inequality present in society's roles and lovers' roles, and the difference is made quite clear when Bertram first describes Lady Geraldine to his friend:

There are none of England's daughters who can show a prouder presence;
Upon princely suitors' praying she has looked in her disdain.
She was sprung of English nobles, I was born of English peasants;
What was *I* that I should love her, save for competence to pain?

I was only a poor poet made for singing at her casement,
As the finches or the thrushes, while she thought of other things.
Oh, she walked so high above me, she appeared to my abasement,
In her lovely silken murmur, like an angel clad in wings!

(2.281–82)

When Bertram considers the social inequality which divides him from Lady Geraldine, his tone is bitter; with those numerous alliterative *p*s, he almost seems to be spitting out his scorn for the system. He is echoing the views of the majority, not his own, but is convinced that these are the views that will prevail; he has little hope of seeing his dream of a more democratic world realized. Gradually, however, the bitterness disappears and is replaced by a sense of wonder and reverence. The language softens as he dwells on a vision of Geraldine, who first appears to him in that highly traditional role of an angel from heaven, silent save for the murmur of her silks. Bertram as social creature may have little use for class distinctions, but as Barrett Browning shows, the experience of romantic love inevitably creates its own set of distinctions, its own levels of inequality. Bertram as poet and lover sees Geraldine as a superior being not because he is dazzled by her wealth and position, but quite simply because he loves her.

The romantic deification of the beloved emerges throughout Bertram's letter. At first, he believes that he loves Geraldine because she is a Platonic form of ideal beauty and he, as a poet, "could not choose but love her" (2.282). "I was born to poet-uses," he tells his friend:

To love all things set above me, all of good and all of fair.
Nymphs of mountain, not of valley, we are wont to call the Muses;
And in nympholeptic climbing, poets pass from mount to star.

(2.282)

But while retaining the concept of worship as a significant part of romantic relationships, Barrett Browning deftly removes her hero from the ranks of such characters as Sir Hubert in "The Romaunt of the Page." When he overhears Geraldine's conversation with the earl, and the hopes that he has unconsciously been harboring are dashed, Bertram recognizes that he has loved Geraldine not just as a "heavenly object"—in the same way that he "loved pure inspirations, loved the graces, loved the virtues" (2.295–96), but also as a woman. Her declaration, therefore, is particularly painful for him; not only does Geraldine confirm his belief that she would never marry such as he, but her apparent arrogance also detracts from his image of her perfect goodness; the beauty seems to be detached from the virtue. His vision of Geraldine no longer appears to match the reality.

Geraldine feels as unworthy of Bertram as he does of her, and is not above indulging in a little nympholepsy herself. She has woods in Sussex, she announces when inviting the young man to Wycombe, with "some purple shades at gloaming / Which are worthy of a king in state, or poet in his youth" (2.284). The royal purple she believes to be equally suited to king and poet, and by directly equating the two, she explicitly reveals her attitude towards Bertram. While he is the lowly poet worshipping the divine lady, she is the young girl adoring the superior soul with his great poet-heart. As they sit among the daisies on the hillside, and Geraldine encourages Bertram to speak on the spirit or pleads with him for a poem, she becomes like a schoolgirl eager to learn from and to please her teacher. And when she finally goes to Bertram's chamber, her sense of unworthiness is unmistakable. "Dost thou, Bertram, truly love me?" she asks in wonder, "Is no woman far above me / Found more worthy of thy poet-heart than such a one as *I?*" (2.309).

The experience of romantic love, Barrett Browning suggests, precludes any possibility of a conviction of equality in a relationship. It is the lover's belief in the infinite superiority of the beloved that results, when love is discovered to be returned, in that elevating sense of wonder which is experienced by both Bertram and Geraldine.

Bertram's angry tirade is the means by which Geraldine learns he returns her love, and it is apparently his declaration of love, not his bitter recriminations, that she primarily hears and to which she eventually responds. When the passionate flow of words abruptly ends, she looks up "as if in wonder, / With tears beaded on her lashes, and said—'Bertram!'—It was all" (2.304). The joyful surprise and wonder experienced by Bertram upon discovering Geraldine loves him are described less directly but in more detail. When Geraldine comes into his chamber—surely a daring step—she is silently smiling, crying, and blushing. She approaches Bertram with "her two white hands extended as if praying one offended, / And a look of supplication gazing earnest in his face" (2.308). There can be little doubt what her presence means. Consequently, Bertram is simply unable to believe that she is really with him. He assumes that he is dreaming, conjuring up a "vision . . . of mercies" (2.307); the implications of her actual presence would be overwhelming. As Geraldine glides closer to him, he desperately clings to his conviction that she is a vision; "No approaching—hush, no breathing!" he pleads, "or my heart must swoon to death in /The too utter life thou bringest, O thou dream of Geraldine!" (2.309). It is only when Geraldine touches him and with "both her hands enfolding both of his" says "Bertram, if I say I love thee, . . . 'tis the vision only speaks" (2.309), that he is forced to acknowledge her actual presence. For both the reader and

Bertram, Geraldine becomes far more than the traditional angelic beloved, passive, silent, and unobtainable in her perfection; the vision and the woman merge.

Although "Lady Geraldine's Courtship" ends with Bertram kneeling before Geraldine in the conventional pose of the lover adoring his lady, for the greater part of the poem he is actually the lover only in the most figurative sense. His letter is full of images commonly associated with love-melancholy. Love is seen as a wound inflicted by Geraldine in the alternately blessed and cursed woods of Sussex. The arrows which inflict the wound come from Geraldine's hypnotic eyes which "undo" Bertram and draw him on, and from her lips "of silent passion, / Curved like an archer's bow to send the bitter arrows out" (2.307–8). Like the most conventional of lovers, Bertram is left "mad and blind" with an almost painfully acute sensitivity to the presence or voice of his beloved (2.285). He reads the poems of Petrarch, among others, to Geraldine and avoids the company of her guests whenever possible, preferring to languish alone and listen to Geraldine's "pure voice o'erfloat the rest" (2.286), or to muse over the poems of Camoens, another lover cruelly separated from his lady by society. There is little that Shakespeare's Rosalind could teach Bertram.

But although Bertram is certainly a perfect literary lover, his only active courting of Geraldine is contained, ironically, in the angry lecture to which he subjects her. As he listens to Lady Geraldine and the earl, he literally sees red (2.300); he feels within him the "conventions coiled to ashes" (2.299), and suddenly becomes quite capable of openly speaking his mind. He reveals not only his anger, but also his love, and his lecture on the equality of all men gradually becomes a series of bitter compliments to Geraldine on her "lovely spirit face" and "voice of holy sweetness" (2.302). As Bertram's passions build and there is no response from Geraldine, he quickly works up to a full declaration of his feelings:

> Have you any answer madam? If my spirit were less earthly
> If its instrument were gifted with a better silver string,
> I would kneel down where I stand, and say—Behold me! I am worthy
> Of thy loving, for I love thee. I am worthy as a king.
>
> (2.303)

This climactic moment is tinged with irony for the reader; Geraldine has already vainly tried to indicate to Bertram that he is indeed, in her eyes, the equal of a king.

Geraldine is far more active in the role of lover than Bertram. She may even be seen as the female version of that noble Duke on a red roan steed that Barrett Browning's earlier heroines, such as Little Ellie and Duchess May, either dream about or love. Bertram, conversely, with his tears, his tenderness, and his sensitivity, displays numerous "feminine" qualities which are appropriate to both lover and beloved. Geraldine's more active role, admittedly, is partly the result of the differences in their social positions. In spite of all Bertram's theories, he could never initiate the relationship. It is essential that Geraldine should make the first move and invite him to Wycombe. Nevertheless, throughout the poem Barrett Browning continually undercuts the importance of social position.

This was, indeed, Coventry Patmore's major objection to the poem. Quite certain that such an ill-matched pair as Geraldine and Bertram could never be happy, Patmore reminds us just how strongly early nineteenth-century society would object to such a "mésalliance." Geraldine would be forced to relinquish her "*station in society,*" he observes with distaste, and this point is not made clearly enough in the poem. If Barrett Browning meant to show the nobility of Geraldine,

> in leaving the condition in which she had passed her life, for the sake of passing it henceforward in the unsophisticated company of an uneducated poet, and his friends and relations, she ought, in order to bring out her meaning artistically, to have shown that the Lady was not only fully aware of the sacrifice she was making, but that she was also capable of enduring it to the end, with all its trying circumstances of social contempt and dissonance of habits.[6]

Patmore is obviously more concerned with the effects of social position than the effects of love. He approaches the relationship of Bertram and Geraldine from a sensible and logical perspective and clearly disapproves of Barrett Browning's romantic conclusion that love conquers all. But while Patmore makes a valid point, he tends to reduce art to life and seems to wish Barrett Browning had written a different poem, a poem—like the later *Aurora Leigh*—in which the various practical problems inherent in a relationship are considered as thoroughly as the emotional responses of the lovers.[7]

Patmore's objection to the marriage, however, is perhaps not based entirely on its social incongruity. One of the distinctions that he makes between Bertram and Geraldine is rather telling: for Bertram to fall in love with an earl's daughter, he declares, is "not wonderful, or out of course; but that she should have fallen in love with and married him is, and we will venture to add, ought to be so."[8] Patmore's logic here seems questionable; he finds Bertram's passion natural, but believes Geraldine's should have been checked. The middle-class reading public, though it could accept the romantic notion of the marriage of a man to his social inferior—a Cinderella or a Pamela—still reacted strongly against the idea of a high-born woman stooping to conquer. This was precisely because such a situation implies an active sexuality on the woman's part. Barrett Browning does not hesitate to create an actively sexual heroine, and despite the grim mutterings of such critics as Patmore and Stedman, she successfully romanticizes the feminine plot of desire. Patmore's objections to the story surely stem partly from his uneasy recognition that Barrett Browning is suggesting that social standing can become unimportant once a woman is permitted to feel normal sexual desire.

As Barrett Browning undercuts the importance of social position in the poem as a whole, so, I believe, she minimizes its significance as a cause of Geraldine's active love-making. Geraldine is a strong woman with an independent mind and a healthy disregard for convention; in courting Bertram she is as defiant as he would be in courting her. And her active wooing is not confined to the obvious examples of inviting Bertram to Wycombe and going to his chamber to declare her love; she attempts to win him in various subtle ways. Once she has the poet at Wycombe, she continues to pay him particular attention. Repeatedly, she coaxes him to join her and her friends, and, when he lingers behind, apparently draws on all her charms to encourage him. Her conversation is always obviously directed to Bertram, and her other guests seem forgotten. In the midst of a large gathering, Geraldine manages to transform the time she spends with Bertram into intimate moments.

This sense of intimacy pervades "Lady Geraldine's Courtship" and clearly reflects Barrett Browning's primary concern with the nature of Bertram and Geraldine's love. The poem may be, as she explained in a letter, "'a romance of the age,' treating of railroads, routes, and all manner of temporalities" (EBB 1.177), but the romance is far more important than the railroads. As Barrett Browning becomes more interested in the intricacies of love than of plot, she also searches for new ways to convey the nature of the love she describes, and, to a great extent, she relies on the effects of highly sensuous language and imagery. The rendering of sensuous experience in "Lady Geraldine's Courtship" becomes a true register of both erotic and emotional attraction, and a means of providing the reader with access to the inner lives of her characters. There is little sensuous description in the early ballads, a telling reflection of the frustration of desire pervading the poems, and when it does occur, it usually suggests desire displaced. There is more of the sensual, for example, in Duchess May's caressing the red roan steed on which she escapes from that abhorrent—yet sexually magnetic—villain, Lord Leigh, than there ever is in her relationship with the stiff picture-book knight she marries.

In "Lady Geraldine's Courtship," an abundance of sensuous description brings the love of the poet and the lady alive for the reader, and it clearly establishes that, despite Bertram's nympholeptic leanings, he does not love an ideal or a vision, but an actual woman. There are two sides to Geraldine's character—the regal, awe-inspiring lady, and the playful, often child-like woman. Bertram apparently finds her highly desirable in both roles. As the high-born lady, Geraldine is kingly, princely, and owns vast properties; it is not her wealth or position that attract Bertram, however, but the power and strength they bestow upon her, her consequent ability to "threaten and command" (2.281). This Geraldine is associated with luxurious surroundings, the "crimson carpet" and the "perfumed air" (2.281), and the finest jewels in the land. When she rejects her numerous suitors, she deals with them as "imperially as Venus did the waves" (2.296). Her demonstration of power and control enables Bertram to feel more acutely her superiority—and the attitude of worship is, for both him and Geraldine, erotically satisfying.

As she demonstrates when inviting Bertram to Wycombe, Geraldine can play the role of the grand lady with great style. She deals with the obvious disapproval of her friends with a "calm and regnant spirit" (2.283), and when she leaves the room, resembles "one who quells the lions" (2.285). Her magnificence leaves Bertram quivering with silent pleasure. Even in this scene, however, she reveals the other side to her character when she softens visibly as she turns to Bertram. Lady Geraldine, lion-tamer, is replaced by Geraldine, lover. Sharp coldness is succeeded by an overflowing warmth, a welcoming smile, and an almost flirtatious tone when she says:

> I invite you, Mister Bertram, to no scene for worldly speeches—
> Sir, I scarce should dare—but only where God asked the thrushes first:
> And if you will sing beside them, in the covert of my beeches,
> I will thank you for the woodlands,—for the human world, at worst.
>
> (2.285)

While Geraldine as lady is most closely associated with courts, castles and ancient halls, Geraldine as woman and lover is associated with these woodlands, with hills, forests, swans, and fawns. She appears as an integral part of the natural sensuous world, and as Bertram writes his letter, the sound of the woods that he connects with Geraldine haunts him as much as her "fair face" and "tender voice" (2.285).

Since it is this face and voice that first drive Bertram "mad and blind" (2.285), it is fitting that his sensuous perceptions of Geraldine are revealed primarily through visual and aural images. The sound of Geraldine as she moves is seductively rendered by such alliterative and onomatopoeic phrases as "lovely silken murmur" and "sudden silken stirring" (2.282, 284). While primarily aural, these images also embrace the tactual, and this mingling of senses is particularly appropriate since the sound of Geraldine is something Bertram *feels* intensely. His vision of Geraldine as angel may initially suggest that he resembles the poet of the traditional romantic lyric with its masculinist plot of distance and desire, but the sensuous imagery that he employs eliminates the traditional sense of separation, and emphasizes instead a sense of intimacy and the unmistakable proximity of a flesh-and-blood woman. Bertram registers an acute, almost physical sensitivity to Geraldine's presence; the sound of her arrival, he records, "touched my inner nature through" (2.284).

Geraldine's voice has a similar effect. Unlike the other women, whose voices Bertram scorns as "low with fashion, not with feeling" (2.286), Geraldine has a "pure" and "tender" voice of "holy sweetness" which turns "common words to grace" (2.302). Her "sudden silver speaking" can leave Bertram weak and helpless, and he is easily bound by her "silver-corded speeches" (2.286). The effect of Geraldine's voice is never shown more clearly than at the climax of his passionate tirade:

> But at last there came a pause. I stood all vibrating with thunder
> Which my soul had used. The silence drew her face up like a call.
> Could you guess what word she uttered? She looked up, as if in wonder
> With tears beaded on her lashes, and said—"Bertram!"—It was all.
>
> (2.303–4)

The passage is reminiscent of Herbert's "The Collar" in which the raving of the rebellious soul ends with a simple call from God. Bertram's violent rush of passion is subdued by a single word. He is struck by the "sense accursed and instant, that if even I spake wisely / I spake basely—using truth, if what I spake indeed was true" (2.305). The sound of Geraldine's voice crushes him; in spite of his previous conviction that his anger is justified, he suddenly instinctively feels he is wrong. Geraldine's feelings for Bertram are obviously conveyed through her voice, and Bertram is therefore left thoroughly confused. The message that he seems to detect in the voice is completely at odds with his rational estimation of the situation. At this climactic moment, it is perhaps not so surprising that he should faint away at Geraldine's feet.

Geraldine's appearance is clearly as captivating as her voice, and Bertram frequently interrupts the flow of his narrative to dwell on the vision of her beauty. Every smile and every movement is lingered over and described in detail; even the movement of her garments is noted when Bertram remembers her wandering in the gardens:

> Thus, her foot upon the new-mown grass, bareheaded, with the flowing
> Of the virginal white vesture gathered closely to her throat,
> And the golden ringlets in her neck just quickened by her going,
> And appearing to breathe sun for air, and doubting if to float,—
>
> With a bunch of dewy maple, which her right hand held above her
> And which trembled a green shadow in betwixt her and the skies.
>
> (2.287)

Once again the tactual emerges. The passage may have a primarily visual appeal, but Bertram still conveys the impression that he is actually feeling the wetness of the maple, the pressure of Geraldine's foot on the grass, and the soft flicker of her hair on her neck—Barrett Browning is already well aware of the potential sexual suggestiveness of hair, and she will use such images to even greater effect in *Sonnets from the Portuguese* and *Aurora Leigh.*

It is the effect of the eyes, however, that is most fully explored in "Lady Geraldine's Courtship." Geraldine's "shining eyes, like antique jewels set in Parian statue-stone," Bertram claims, "undo" him (2.307). That steady serene glance which can quell in a moment can also appear soft and inviting. When she turns and looks at Bertram, he remembers, "she drew me on to love her /And to worship the divineness of the smile hid in her eyes" (2.287). Those deep blue eyes "smile constantly, as if they in discreetness / Kept the secret of a happy dream she did not care to speak" (2.288). Geraldine's eyes, like her voice, reveal her love, and Bertram consequently finds her glances a mystery.

The visual and the aural finally become merged in the description of Geraldine singing. As Bertram and Geraldine sit alone on the hillside, they often tire of books and grow silent. The silence gives Bertram a pleasant, yet disconcerting, awareness of Geraldine's presence which is felt with "beatings at the breast" (2.292). Geraldine, apparently similarly disturbed, breaks the silence by bursting into song. "Oh, to see or hear her singing!" Bertram writes,

> scarce I know which is divinest,
> For her looks sing too—she modulates her gestures on the tune,
> And her mouth stirs with the song, like song; and when the notes are finest,
> 'Tis the eyes that shoot out vocal light and seem to swell them on.
>
> Then we talked—oh, how we talked! her voice so cadenced in the talking,
> Made another singing—of the soul! a music without bars.
>
> (2.293)

Geraldine herself becomes the song, and what is sung is indistinguishable from the singer; Bertram responds with the senses and the spirit.

Both the presentation of Geraldine as song and singer and the mingling of the sensuous and the spiritual in this central passage become a reflection of Barrett Browning's larger concern within the poem to create and celebrate a successful romantic relationship. The lines which traditionally divide poet from lady, subject from object, lover from beloved, and sensuous from spiritual gradually dissolve, and, as they do, the barriers which left Barrett Browning's earlier heroines frustrated, able to find satisfaction only by accepting God as substitute beloved, are overcome. Barrett Browning may employ a relatively conventional form, situation, and speaker, but she deftly subverts the surface conventions, and the sub-text gradually emerges to dominate the poem. A forceful female voice speaks of love, the heroine assumes an active role in the relationship, and an abundance of sensuous imagery suggests both erotic and emotional attraction. As Barrett Browning's first detailed evocation and dramatization of a growing love, "Lady Geraldine's Courtship" consequently marks a crucial turning point between the early ballads, with their emphasis on the frustration of desire and their frequently superficial treatment of emotional relationships, and such later works as *Sonnets from the Portuguese* and *Aurora Leigh* with their more mature and complex investigation of the experience of love.

4

Space and Distance: The Dramatization of Desire in *Sonnets from the Portuguese*

Edmund Stedman spoke for the majority of Victorians when he pronounced the *Sonnets from the Portuguese* to be Barrett Browning's finest work; these poems, he claimed,

> whose title was a screen behind which the singer poured out her full heart, are the most exquisite poetry hitherto written by a woman, and of themselves justify us in pronouncing their author the greatest of her sex—on the ground that the highest mission of a female poet is the expression of love, and that no other woman approaching her in genius has essayed the ultimate form of the expression.[1]

The manner in which Stedman evaluates the sonnets is typical of nineteenth-century criticism. Many of Barrett Browning's readers still believed that the function of woman was "not to write, not to act, not to be famous—but to love";[2] if she insisted on writing, however, she could be forgiven if she restricted herself to woman's domain and wrote of personal love; this was not really considered art, but simply a confessional flow of emotion. Not surprisingly, the poetic merits of the sequence were usually ignored; critics based their appreciation of the poems on the grounds that they were "the outpouring of a woman's tenderest emotions," that they revealed the "woman more than the poet," and that they provided the voyeuristic pleasure of seeing the "innermost secrets of another heart laid bare."[3] Praise for the *Sonnets from the Portuguese* reached an enthusiastic pitch primarily because the poems were seen as the sincere and spontaneous expression of Barrett Browning's personal emotional experiences.

The popularity of the sonnets has declined dramatically during the past fifty years. They are now often ridiculed or ignored, and critics frequently claim that reading these love poems leaves them "uncomfortable" or "embarrassed."[4] According to Alethea Hayter, they are not Barrett Browning's best work "because in them she is dealing with an emotion too new and powerful for her to transmute it into universally valid terms . . . one has Peeping Tom sensations."[5]

Our assessment of the poems may be quite different from the Victorians', but the grounds on which we base our assessment seem to remain much the same. It is rather discomfiting to find some critics still claiming, in all apparent seriousness, that the sonnets contain "the spontaneous outpouring of private love."[6] Apparently we have still not quite shaken off the myth that when women write of love it is necessarily instinctive and personal. A knowledge of Barrett Browning's life and letters may illuminate the work, but our appreciation and understanding of Barrett Browning as a poet, rather than as a woman, will continue to be restricted as long as there is an insistence on viewing the *Sonnets from the Portuguese* as the documented story of an actual romance instead of a series of finely crafted poems.

As well as being considered too personal, the sonnets are now also frequently condemned for being overly self-deprecating.[7] Love poetry is filled with protestations of unworthiness, however, and it is questionable whether a work should be criticized simply because the speaker indulges in self-deprecation. The stance to be found in troubadour verse is considered by many to be disturbingly perverse, and we might prefer to believe that Shakespeare did not really view himself in the manner implied by such lines as "Being your slave, what should I do but tend / Upon the hours and times of your desire." But it is not necessarily a requirement that poetry be such as we approve of as "normal" or "healthy," and if these poets were stripped of their potentially "offensive" ideologies, it is doubtful that their poetry would remain as effective. They exploit the stance of self-deprecation for specific dramatic effects, and the aesthetic dimension must be considered along with the ideological.

Similarly, when a woman experiences a robust and healthy love for a man she considers her equal, we may have an entirely satisfactory situation in life, but we might not have such a stimulating and dramatically effective situation for poetry. When the poet is a woman, of course, the situation inevitably becomes more complex. Barrett Browning's stance of self-deprecation in *Sonnets from the Portuguese* is immediately suspect since she may be seen to reinforce woman's role as subordinate, other, inessential. But if the aesthetic dimension of the role is considered as well as the ideological, it becomes apparent not only that she is assuming the stance for specific dramatic effects, but that one of these effects is the subversion of what might superficially appear as the dominant ideology of the sonnets: the woman who speaks actually emerges as a strong and active lover. Barrett Browning appropriates a number of sonnet conventions and adapts them in order to delineate a form of love quite different from that which the conventions would typically suggest. It is, therefore, the particularly dramatic value of Barrett Browning's stance, of her role-playing, which now remains in need of further evaluation and which will lead to a clearer understanding of her accomplishments as a poet.

The two major complaints against the *Sonnets from the Portuguese*—that they are too personal and overly self-deprecating—are closely related. Barrett Browning does indeed often refer to what appears to be her personal situation—her pale cheeks, trembling hands, heavy heart, constant weeping, and unnatural isolation—and she does this in order to stress her unworthiness. The story to be extracted from the sonnets is, to a great extent, responsible for the creation of the Browning myth, and it is quite understandable that nineteenth-century reviewers, reading these poems, tended to speculate with wild surges of romantic enthusiasm about the "broken body and broken heart of the sweet singer, Elizabeth Barrett,"[8] and to assure their readers that this real-life Sleeping Beauty "lived a dreamy, solitary life, a prisoner in the sick chamber, till Love came to create new life within her and draw her once more out into the world."[9] This is, after all, a fairly accurate transcription of what Barrett Browning tells us in her sonnets.

It is difficult to determine, however, the extent to which this reflects Barrett Browning's actual situation, the extent to which it is a created role, or the extent to which it is a role both created and lived. Romantic rumors concerning Barrett Browning's life emerged even before the advent of Robert Browning, and were first "confirmed" for the public by her correspondent R. H. Horne. Barrett Browning collaborated with Horne on *A New Spirit of the Age* (1844), and when he wrote a chapter on Caroline Norton and Barrett Browning, Horne could not resist confiding to his audience that the

> latter lady, or "fair shade"—whichever she may be—is not known personally to anybody, we had almost said; but her poetry is known to a highly intellectual class, and she "lives" in constant correspondence with many of the most eminent persons of the time. . . . Confined entirely to her own apartment, and almost hermetically sealed, in consequence of some extremely delicate state of health, the poetess of whom we write is scarcely ever seen by any but her own family.[10]

The "fair shade" was both irritated—"mere romancing!" she snapped—by this account,[11] and amused. To Mr. Westwood she wryly observed:

> I have not been shut up in the dark for seven years by any manner of means. . . . [A] barrister said to my barrister brother the other day, "I suppose your sister is dead?" "Dead?" said he, a little struck; "dead?" "Why, yes. After Mr. Horne's account of her being sealed up hermetically in the dark for so many years, one can only calculate upon her being dead by this time." (EBB 1.174)

But no matter how much she protested against such romancing, as Daniel Karlin persuasively demonstrates, Barrett Browning herself, "in her published writings as well as her letters, strengthened the image of herself as incurable and inconsolable."[12] Vague tantalizing references in prefaces and dedications to her poetry being "shadowed, by the life of which they are the natural expression," and to her "saddest and sweetest past" (2.143; 2.142) invite sentimental conjecture. "Part of her status as a writer arose, inevitably, from the mystery of her suffering and isolation," as Karlin notes, and "she cultivated this mystery."[13]

Barrett Browning has for too long been considered an intensely subjective poet; as such works as "Bertha in the Lane" and "Lady Geraldine's Courtship" prove, she was as capable as Browning of assuming a mask and playing a role. The persona speaking in the *Sonnets from the Portuguese* is obviously not a completely separate and detached character in the manner of Bertram or elder sister, nor is it just Barrett Browning; it is Barrett Browning playing a role. To create this role she exploits many elements of her own character and situation, but it is no less a role for that; the elements are continually heightened, transformed, and skillfully exploited for specific dramatic effects. To indicate this mixture of detachment and involvement in the speaker of the sonnets—and to distinguish her from Barrett Browning as poet and Barrett Browning as writer of the love letters—I shall refer to her simply as she or the speaker and to the man addressed as he or the beloved.

According to Angela Leighton, "to free Barrett Browning's name from the web of pious legend and sweet romance that has entangled it for so long must be the first task of any new critical evaluation."[14] While generally agreeing with Leighton, I would add that, particularly in the case of the sonnets, it is also necessary to determine why Barrett Browning herself frequently "cultivated the mystery" and perpetuated the myths. Leighton herself provides one answer when she responds to those critics who reject the sonnets as overly self-deprecating. There is a "subtle competition" between Robert and Elizabeth "to be the lover, not the beloved," Leighton writes, and the speaker's insistence on offering herself as one of the "meanest creatures" to a god stems from Barrett Browning's determination to write as the unworthy lover who speaks, traditionally the male role, rather than the superior but passive and silent beloved, traditionally the female role. "To see only the self-deprecation of her confessed unworthiness is to miss the proud assertion of her accompanying rights, 'to love you better than I could do if I were more worthy to be loved by you.'"[15] Dorothy Mermin makes a similar point when she examines the "blurring of sexual roles" in the sonnets. The female speaker, Mermin believes, by filling roles that "earlier love poetry had kept separate and opposite: speaker and listener, subject and object of desire, male and female," determines the standard response to the poems. The reader's "first overwhelming though inaccurate impression of the poems is that they are awkward, mawkish, and indecently personal—in short, embarrassing."[16] As both Leighton and Mermin convincingly show, Barrett Browning exploits her "personal" situation, her "unworthiness," to claim the stronger role of the lover and—by inference—to claim the voice of the poet.

The role that Barrett Browning plays in *Sonnets from the Portuguese* is one important aspect of her attempt to appropriate and adapt the sonnet in order to accommodate the female lyric voice of desire. All the problems that women poets face in writing lyric become intensified when they turn more specifically to the traditionally male-dominated sonnet sequence and write in the shadow of such poets as Petrarch, Dante, Sidney, and Shakespeare. Instead of simply attempting to speak from the position of the conventionally silent and passive beloved, to speak as a Laura, a Beatrice, a Stella, or her own Catarina, and only *respond* to the lover's passion, Barrett Browning confounds the traditional roles of lover and beloved—as she previously did in "Lady Geraldine's Court-ship"—and the speaker alternately appears as both active speaking subject and silent passive object. She offers herself as the poetic object of his verse (17) and as the visual object of her own (10).[17] She appears as the passive beloved unable to respond to the pleading lover: "let the silence of my womanhood / Commend my woman-love to thy belief,— / Seeing that I stand unwon, however wooed" (13). Simultaneously, however, she is the pale, weary lover who weeps, trem-bles, and pleads, the "poor tired wandering singer" (3) who exalts and celebrates her beloved in verse, and joyfully counts the ways in which she loves. And it is this active and vocal role of lover which predominates. Female desire is directly and forcefully expressed.

In the traditional male lyric, the roles of lover and beloved and the desire of the speaker for the object of his love are primarily dramatized by the trope of distance. Barrett Browning follows tradition in this respect, and by using her personal situation and stressing her unworthiness she imposes the necessary distance between the speaker and the beloved. There is a notable difference, however, in the manner in which she exploits the trope of distance to dramatize the speaker's desire. The male lyric typically relies upon distance to impose a space between lover and unattainable beloved which is never actually traversed; the lover *views* his beloved across this space, and frustrated desire is expressed primarily with the use of visual metaphor. A number of recent critics have suggested that women's love poetry, in contrast, depends more upon the tactual than the visual. According to Luce Irigaray:

> Woman's desire would not be expected to speak the same language as man's; woman's desire has doubtless been submerged by the logic that has dominated the West since the time of the Greeks.
>
> Within this logic, the predominance of the visual, and of the discrimination and individu-alization of form, is particularly foreign to female eroticism. Woman takes pleasure more from touching than from looking, and her entry into a dominant scopic economy signifies, again, her consignment to passivity: she is to be the beautiful object of contemplation.[18]

Barrett Browning's use of the trope of distance in *Sonnets from the Portuguese* certainly supports the general view of woman's preference for the tactual rather than the visual.[19] Throughout the sequence there is the sense of distance being overcome, space being eliminated, and of the sensuous touching and joining of lovers. There are two major clusters of images based on the concept of space and distance in these sonnets, and both are used by Barrett Browning to express and develop role, to dramatize desire, and to suggest the speaker's movement towards an acceptance and celebration of a love which rejoices in the physical and the sensuous. The first group focuses on breadth, on separation and union, and the second on heights and depths, on ascent and descent. It is surely no accident that in the best-known sonnet the speaker begins counting the ways with the line "I love thee to the depth and breadth and height / My soul can reach" (43).

In the opening sonnets, which enumerate the various obstacles to love, distance is employed both literally and metaphorically as the speaker attempts to convince the beloved—and herself—that their love, their union, is impossible. At first, the major obstacle appears to be some rather mysterious divine decree; the distance God has put between them, she claims, is insurmountable:

> "Nay" is worse
> From God than from all others, O my friend!
> Men could not part us with their worldly jars,
> Nor the seas change us, nor the tempests bend;
> Our hands would touch for all the mountain bars,—
> And, heaven being rolled between us at the end,
> We should but vow the faster for the stars.
>
> (2)

Despite the conditional premise of her declaration, this is a remarkably passionate and vigorous avowal of love. The very thought of separation and the notion of distance needing to be overcome appear to make the desire which she must repress more urgent and the regret which she reveals more poignant.

Attempting to explain the restrictions against their love further, she claims that they are bound to remain apart because of the differences in their "uses" and "destinies" (3); to clarify her meaning and dramatize the metaphorical distance between them, she begins to place herself and the beloved in a variety of roles. He is the "chief musician" (3), the most "gracious singer of high poems" (4), and he belongs on some palace floor where he will cast his spell over the dancers and capture the hearts of all who listen (4). She is only the "poor, tired, wandering singer" (3) whom he watches from a distance through the window as, leaning against a cypress tree, she sings through the dark (3). At this point, notably, where she speaks of desire resisted, not consummated, the more traditional visual image predominates. While the beloved belongs amid the warm glittering world of society, she, like Tennyson's "Mariana," is surrounded by ruins:

Look up and see the casement broken in,
The bats and owlets builders in the roof!
My cricket chirps against thy mandolin.
Hush, call no echo up in further proof
Of desolation! there's a voice within
That weeps...as thou must sing...alone, aloof.

(4)

Although Barrett Browning is certainly not giving a literal description of herself in these early sonnets, elements of her own character and situation are nevertheless being exploited, in a transformed state, to dramatize the various roles assumed by the speaker. The speaker's humility and morbidity, to which modern readers are apt to object, are in splendid contrast to the confident and princely virility of the beloved. Through this contrast, Barrett Browning introduces the idea of the distance which is, in one form or another, the necessary impediment in all great love stories—Montague and Capulet, Rochester and Jane, Prince and Cinderella, queen and knight, and god and mortal. Emphasis on the difference and the distance between lovers inevitably leads the consummation, when it occurs, to appear all the more moving and perfect.

But while exploiting this tradition, Barrett Browning simultaneously undermines it. The desire and regret that she expresses so fiercely in these early sonnets are complicated by the presence of other emotions; when she claims that she must remain "alone, aloof," the choice of the word "aloof" is telling. Although on one level the beloved appears more princely and the music he drops in voluptuous "folds of golden fulness" at her door more appealing because of the contrast with her desolation and bitter tears (4), there is also an unmistakable hint of pride in the speaker's self-portrait. When she opens sonnet 3 with the claim "Unlike are we, unlike, O princely Heart / Unlike our uses and our destinies," it is unclear whether the lines are colored only by regret, or if they are also tinged with a touch of self-satisfaction. She does appear to envision herself as a rather romantic figure, romantic in much the same way, perhaps, as the operatic consumptive who fades so movingly into death with one final anguished aria. The implications of her question "What hast *thou* to do / With looking from the lattice-lights at me" consequently become rather ambiguous (3).[20] He may be involved in an active social world, but this could be considered a touch frivolous. She may know nothing of society, but she has long been familiar with the dark secrets of grief, isolation, and death. He is the public poet, she the interpreter of the sorrowful heart and soul—it is difficult to be certain which role she considers to be superior.

The cause of her ambivalence is suggested in the opening sonnet which records the arrival of love in her life. Before meeting the beloved, she has accepted and even become relatively content with her sorrows; she has, as Alethea Hayter notes, created for herself a "hiding place, a living grave, snow-cold but quiet and safe."[21] She recalls a moment in which she quietly mused over these past griefs:

> I thought once how Theocritus had sung
> Of the sweet years, the dear and wished for years,
> Who each one in a gracious hand appears
> To bear a gift for mortals, old or young:
> And, as I mused it in his antique tongue,
> I saw, in gradual vision through my tears,
> The sweet, sad years, the melancholy years,
> Those of my own life, who by turns had flung
> A shadow across me.

(1)

Although the past years have brought no joy, there is little suggestion of dissatisfaction and certainly no resentment or rebellion in these opening lines. That shadow which has been flung over her is somehow comforting; it has provided her with a peaceful retreat from the world. There is a dangerous seductive attraction in such protected placidity, and, as the hypnotic repetition in such lines as "the sweet years, the dear and wished for years," and "the sweet, sad years, the melancholy years" suggests, she has gradually been lulled into drowsy quiescence by the silky caresses of sorrow; she has grown to take some pride in her situation and thinks only to "sink" into death (7). Once again, Barrett Browning dramatizes the attractions of withdrawal from the world.

The speaker is jolted out of her trance-like state by the advent of Love. This "mystic shape" which silently creeps up behind her turns out to be a powerful and physical force (1), and her first encounter with this force is described with a strikingly tactual image. She is seized violently by the hair and, in the grip of this new emotion, drawn backwards away from the vision of her past, forced out of her passivity, and compelled to struggle in the masterful hold of new and disturbing feelings. Fear, therefore, appears to have much to do with her initial desperate attempts to keep the beloved at a distance. He threatens to come between her and the peaceful death which for all these years has been the only focus of her desire.

The various roles that the speaker enacts in the opening sonnets nevertheless fail to deter the beloved; he has the ability, as she later notes, to "look through and behind this mask of me" (39). In the face of his persistence, she changes her tactics. Instead of trying to convince him that they are simply too unlike, she suggests that if her passion is encouraged, she might become dangerous. Now she moves into the role of a tragic Greek heroine:

> I lift my heavy heart up solemnly,
> As once Electra her sepulchral urn,

And, looking in thine eyes, I overturn
The ashes at thy feet. Behold and see
What a great heap of grief lay hid in me,
And how the red wild sparkles dimly burn
Through the ashen greyness.

(5)

It is the embers of passion, not the ashes of grief, which now dictate that they should remain apart. The closeness of the beloved is stirring these ashes, and if they burst into flame, she warns,

those laurels on thine head,
O my Belovèd, will not shield thee so,
That none of all the fires shall scorch and shred
The hair beneath. Stand further off then! go.

(5)

The change from the "O my friend" of sonnet 2 to the "O my beloved" of sonnet 5 is telling. Although the speaker's voice is becoming more insistent that he should depart, she is simultaneously becoming more aware that this is not what she actually desires. She is changing the focus of her desire, moving away from a solipsistic fascination with grief, isolation, and prospective death towards an eager acceptance, then a subsequent celebration, of the more vigorous and physical attractions of life, love, and the beloved.

The listing of various obstacles to their union seems to reach a climax when the commanding voice which closes sonnet 5 re-emerges in the curt and forceful opening line of sonnet 6: "Go from me." But the effect of this blunt and decisive final decree is completely confounded by an immediate "Yet," and in the following lines the speaker reveals her awareness that she and the beloved will never be separated again. The idea that distance makes love impossible is replaced by the conviction that love makes distance impossible. The shadow formerly flung over her by the unhappy past has been replaced by the shadow of the beloved; and like the "mystic Shape" of sonnet 1, this brooding shadow has an intensely physical presence:

Nevermore
Alone upon the threshold of my door
Of individual life, I shall command
The uses of my soul, nor lift my hand
Serenely in the sunshine as before,
Without the sense of that which I forbore—
Thy touch upon the palm.

(6)

Both the abstract and momentous and the concrete and mundane aspects of her life will now always be marked by that simple sense of his touch. As Carol McGinnis Kay has shown, the entire sonnet is highly sensuous; the speaker feels and senses rather than thinks, and what she feels is that she will never be able to cast off the awareness of his physical presence:[22]

> The widest land
> Doom takes to part us, leaves thy heart in mine
> With pulses that beat double. What I do
> And what I dream include thee, as the wine
> Must taste of its own grapes.
>
> (6)

At the same time as she imagines a future separation of their actual bodies, the speaker can envisage and linger sensuously over the extraordinary knitting together of their whole identities. And this is certainly not a merely cerebral platonism that she describes; this is a tactual union which is as intimate and sensual as a mingling of their actual bodies. With such images as these, it is difficult to understand how Alethea Hayter could conclude with disappoint-ment that the sonnets are "hardly sensual at all."[23] The earthy forcefulness of the image of wine and grapes and the sensuous intimacy of the hearts beating together strikingly anticipate the manner in which love will continue to be characterized within the remaining sonnets. In spite of all the references to spirits, angels, and heavenly thrones, the love that is celebrated in the *Sonnets from the Portuguese* is intensely physical and highly sensuous.

Instead of desiring to maintain distance between herself and the beloved, the speaker now craves complete union. An abundance of such possessives as "My love, my own" serves to draw them together linguistically (38), and the commands "Go from me" and "Stand farther off" are replaced by demands for closeness; she entreats "instantly, / Renew thy presence" (29), or pleads,

> Keep near and close,
> Thou dovelike help! and, when my fears would rise,
> With thy broad heart serenely interpose.
> Brood down with thy divine sufficiencies
> These thoughts which tremble when bereft of those,
> Like callow birds left desert to the skies.
>
> (31)

The sharp fear of the unprotected fledglings trembling in the nest is well-captured by the harshness of "callow" and "skies," and the comfort and shelter the bird provides by the soothing long vowels of "broad" and "brood." This

intensely tactual description skillfully conveys the sense of the warm, soft re-
treat that the speaker has come to associate with love.

Such imagery is particularly appropriate since, when she describes her life
before she loved, she often suggests her desolation with references to bleak
wide-open spaces. Even before the speaker recognizes how little comfort and
security is provided by the shadow of sorrow, the reader can easily deduce her
self-delusion from the frequency with which she depicts herself outside in the
cold and dark, unprotected from the elements. She is the wandering minstrel
shut out from the warmth and brightness of the world in which he sings, a
"Mariana" sitting among ruins open to the sky, or Electra waiting for the winds
to blow up the ashes. When she does recognize the true desolation of her world,
the sense of bleakness grows even stronger; she considers herself as having been
thrown on the "drear flat of earth" (27), or, reflecting her previous morbid
preoccupation with her own sorrows, pictures herself sitting alone, counting
her chains, in a chilling, alien world of snow (20).

While her desolation and isolation are conveyed with cold, hard images
and visions of windswept spaces, the satisfactions that love provides are de-
picted with numerous images of warm comforting spaces in which speaker can
be completely enclosed; some of the most effective lines in the sequence result
from the expression of her desire for enclosure, her desire for a place where love
becomes intensely concentrated. Sometimes it is the beloved who provides this
enclosure; "Open thine heart wide," she asks, returning once more to the image
of the soft brooding bird, "And fold within the wet wings of thy dove" (35).
Sometimes, as in sonnet 24, love itself is the shelter in which they are both
subsumed:

> Let the world's sharpness, like a clasping knife
> Shut in upon itself and do no harm
> In this close hand of Love, now soft and warm,
> And let us hear no sound of human strife
> After the click of the shutting. Life to life—
> I lean upon thee, Dear, without alarm,
> And feel as safe as guarded by a charm
> Against the stab of worldlings.
>
> (24)

The unaffected diction, the onomatopoeic effects of the clicking, and the sense
of absolute peace and contentment that she creates with such deceptive ease
make the opening image in these lines a perfect example of how Barrett Brown-
ing can, when she chooses, express herself with both simplicity and precision.

While there is little sense of any actual distance between the lovers after
sonnet 6, the speaker continues to enforce a metaphorical distance throughout
the sonnets by devaluing herself and idealizing her beloved. This is not, how-

ever, in order to place a barrier between them; rather, she is exploiting a stratagem which can be frequently found in writings of romantic love. Stendhal provides one useful summary of the general concept: "the moment he is in love," Stendhal observes, "the steadiest man sees no object such as it is. His own advantages he minimizes, and magnifies the smallest favors of the loved one." This process, to which he gives the name "crystallization," is "the product of human nature, which commands us to enjoy and sends warm blood rushing to our brain; it springs from the conviction that the pleasures of love increase with the perfections of its object."[24] Distance, as usual, intensifies desire.

For Barrett Browning, as for many of her characters, the erotic satisfaction to be derived from the romantic relationship is intensified to a painfully thrilling degree by dwelling on the superiority of the beloved object. This results in the speaker's powerfully sensuous response to the beloved; we are continually aware of the rushing of warm blood. The heightening of erotic excitement by this process is evident throughout many of the sonnets; but the point is perhaps best illustrated by the two poems recording the exchange of locks of hair, since in this respect they function as a synecdochic expression of much of the sequence, and furthermore, since the exchange is so well-documented in the love-letters, they provide one interesting example of how Barrett Browning transforms experience into art.

The giving and receiving of locks of hair are acts fraught with sexual connotations, with suggestions of sexual yielding, and the love-letters clearly reveal that both Elizabeth and Robert were well aware of the implications of their exchange.[25] "Give me, dearest beyond expression," Browning wrote, tantalizingly delaying the moment when he must specify exactly what it was he desired, "what I have always dared to think I would ask you for...one day! . . . give me so much of you—all precious that you are—as may be given in a lock of your hair—I will live and die with it" (RB 1.288). And she replied:

> I never gave away what you ask me to give *you*, to a human being, except my nearest relatives and once or twice or thrice to female friends,...never, though reproached for it,—and it is just three weeks since I said last to an asker that I was "too great a prude for such a thing"! it was best to anticipate the accusation!—And, prude or not, I could not—I never could—*something* would not let me. And now...what am I to do..."for my sake and not yours"? Should you have it, or not? Why, I suppose...YES...I suppose you must have it. (RB 1.289–90)

Barrett Browning's response contains a curious mixture of the knowing and the coy. The indirection, the teasing hesitation, the reference to prudishness, that mysterious "*something,*" and the simple acceptance of the importance of the gift inherent in "I never gave away what you ask me to give *you*, to a human being," suggests a full awareness of exactly what it is she is being asked to surrender. But then we are left with "except my nearest relatives and once or twice or thrice to female friends." The sexually explosive situation that she creates, she also defuses with the introduction of the humdrum, the reference to girlishly innocent memories. Eventually she gives in, but she demands that he respond in kind: "It shall be pure merchandise or nothing at all" (RB 1.291). The contrast which is suggested in this letter between giving a lock to relatives or female friends and giving a lock to *a man,* particularly this man, points up her awareness that this is now a sexual act. As with Donne's flea, the exchange transforms the hair into "Our marriage bed, and marriage temple . . . / . . . we'are met, / And cloistered in these living walls of jet."

When Barrett Browning translates the exchange into art—one sonnet on her lock, a second on his—the tone created by her reference to friends and relatives dominates the first poem; the hint of sexual teasing is quite absent when she offers that much coveted lock of hair:

> I never gave a lock of hair away
> To a man, Dearest, except this to thee,
> Which now upon my fingers thoughtfully,
> I ring out to the full brown length and say
> "Take it."

                                                                              (18)

The offer seems rather de-eroticized. The words and images that she uses are relatively short and plain; her tone is serious and subdued. This is ordinary, even domestic, speech to suit an ordinary lock of plain brown hair, and her injunction "Take it" is spare and abrupt; there is no teasing hesitation. In much the same way that the two sonnets become a synecdochic expression of much of the sequence, the two locks of hair become a synecdochic expression of the lovers: locks substitute for bodies. Her hair has lost the abundance and vitality that it possessed in her youth:

> It only may
> Now shade on two pale cheeks the mark of tears,
> Taught drooping from the head that hangs aside
> Through sorrow's trick. I thought the funeral-shears
> Would take this first, but Love is justified.

                                                                              (18)

The lock of hair, imbued with her own characteristics, becomes a reminder of age, of sorrow, and, finally, more a *memento mori* than the love token for which he asks. "Take it thou," she finally repeats, "finding pure, from all those years, / The kiss my mother left here when she died" (18). With the rather morbid thought that she gives him, along with her hair, the kiss of a dead woman, the act is purified, even sterilized, of its obvious sexual connotations. The very act of giving a man her lock, however, means that sensuality remains, even if it is subsumed, and when she receives his lock and the exchange is complete, the resulting union is conceived in highly sensual terms.

The sonnet in which she receives his curl is full of joyful voluptuous pleasure:

> The soul's Rialto hath its merchandise;
> I barter curl for curl upon that mart,
> And from my poet's forehead to my heart
> Receive this lock which outweighs argosies,—
> As purply black, as erst to Pindar's eyes,
> The dim purpureal tresses gloomed athwart
> The nine white Muse-brows.
>
> (19)

This is obviously no ordinary lock of hair. The plain spare language of the previous sonnet is replaced by a wealth of romantic literary and classical allusions, the abruptness by a mounting enveloping sense of wonder. He is frequently associated throughout the sequence with the royal purple, and here even his hair reflects his nobility. As she repeatedly dwells on the vibrant hue of this priceless gift, which is "so black!" (19), she reveals the vigor, potency, and physical attractiveness of the man from whom the lock is derived. The kiss that she places on his hair, as she lingers caressingly over its beauty, suggests a sensuously langorous love, not a deathly maternal affection. Capturing the essence of his strength and vitality by harnessing the shade of the bay crown which seems to hover over the lock, she takes him completely to her heart:

> Thus, with a fillet of smooth-kissing breath,
> I tie the shadows safe from gliding back,
> And lay the gift where nothing hindereth;
> Here on my heart, as on thy brow, to lack
> No natural heat till mine grows cold in death.
>
> (19)

As she lays the lock on her bare breast, the importance of the use of synecdoche becomes particularly apparent; the figure allows for the expression of a sexuality that cannot be overtly described (locks may intertwine; bodies may not), and the heat of her body, the heat of her desire, can consequently be transferred to him in a manner that is all the more suggestively erotic because of its very indirection.

Throughout the sonnet sequence, the beloved is characterized in much the same way as in the sonnet describing his lock. He is constantly described in sensuous terms, associated with rich golds and purples, soothing melodies, warm revitalizing breath, and a wide enfolding heart. He is compared to a strong palm tree, a tree which signifies not only victory, but also fertility and abundance. When the speaker's thoughts of the beloved become like wild vines twining around the tree and threaten to stifle the actual man, she calls upon him to renew his presence with an image full of masculine force and vigor:

> As a strong tree should,
> Rustle thy boughs and set thy trunk all bare,
> And let these bands of greenery which insphere thee,
> Drop heavily down,—burst, shattered, everywhere!
> Because, in this deep joy to see and hear thee
> And breathe within thy shadow a new air,
> I do not think of thee—I am too near thee.
>
> (29)

It is frequently observed that in the *Sonnets from the Portuguese*, the beloved is *identified* with God and presented as a divine savior.[26] It would be more accurate to say that he *replaces* God and is presented in a very human form with an intensely physical appeal. In the one sonnet where the beloved comes closest to assuming some divine form and breathes life into the speaker (27), she expresses her wonder with the ultimate compliment: "My own, my own, / Who camest to me when the world was gone, / And I who looked for only God, found *thee!*" (27). The telling placement of "only" and the emphasis on *"thee"* leaves us with no doubt that the new savior is superior to the old.

And the speaker is well aware that the image she has created of the beloved has a vital physical appeal. In sonnet 37 she apologizes for her inability to capture his "strong divineness" adequately, but her apology seems somewhat tongue in cheek.[27] She compares herself to a "shipwrecked Pagan" who,

> safe in port,
> His guardian sea-god to commemorate,
> Should set a sculptured porpoise, gills a-snort
> And vibrant tail, within the temple-gate.
>
> (37)

It is as a man, with all the erotic attractions suggested by the porpoise's snorting gills and vibrant tail, not as some divine spiritual being, that the beloved comes alive for the reader in these poems—and it is clearly the man, not the divine essence, who holds the primary appeal for the speaker.

While the beloved is characterized with an abundance of sensory detail, it is usually through the absence of such detail—as in the sonnet on her lock—that the speaker characterizes herself in the early poems. When she does use sensuous images, she manages to convey a sense of deathliness rather than vitality. She is associated with dust, poison, ashes, bitter salt tears, and grave-damps. He is the splashing porpoise, she "a bee shut in a crystalline" (15), and such a lifeless object, she regrets, is quite incapable of shattering the glass of its prison; "to spread wing and fly in the outer air / Were most impossible failure" (15). In return for the priceless golds and purples of his heart, she can offer nothing of value:

> Frequent tears have run
> The colours from my life, and left so dead
> And pale a stuff, it were not fitly done
> To give the same as pillow to thy head.
> Go farther! let it serve to trample on.
>
>   (8)

The excessive self-abasement in these lines may be disturbing, but it does, in its angry rejection of her faded, sterile life, suggest the potential vigor and strength within her waiting to be released.

And the sonnets are frequently marked by the image of life springing out of death, of apparently inanimate objects becoming infused with a new vitality. Out of the darkness of winter comes the "fresh Spring in all her green completed" (21); her letters, mute dead white paper, become "alive and quivering" within her "tremulous hands" (28); and, in the most striking of all the images of animation, her pilgrim's staff, an austere symbol of asceticism, bursts into life; with the sudden budding of wet green leaves, the barren becomes fertile (42).

Like these objects, the speaker is gradually animated and invigorated under the influence of love. Significantly, although she has characterized herself with the absence of sensory detail, the love that she begins to recognize within herself is highly sensuous. As she tells the beloved, she may be poor, but she is certainly not "cold" (8). Her passion is frequently referred to as a fire, and this love, this fire, can transform her:

> Fire is bright,
> Let temple burn, or flax; an equal light
> Leaps in the flame from cedar-plank or weed:
> And love is fire. And when I say at need
> *I love thee...mark!...I love thee!*—in thy sight
> I stand transfigured.
>
>   (10)

As Angela Leighton observes of this sonnet, it is important to recognize that "the change comes from within. . . . The poem does not invoke the presence or the attention or the reciprocity of the loved object in order to be 'worthy.'"[28] The speaker brings about her own transformation simply by allowing herself to love: "what I *feel*, across the inferior features / Of what I *am*, doth flash itself, and show / How that great work of Love enhances Nature's" (10). Although at first she fears that only death will bring them to the same level, she soon learns that "Love, as strong as Death, retrieves as well" (27).

It is the beloved, however, who has, through loving the speaker, prompted her to turn away from death and focus her desire upon him; he provides her with the strength and vitality necessary to effect her own transformation. The beloved brings life to the speaker in much the same way as God brings life to the earth. To suggest the means by which she is invigorated, the speaker begins to exploit the language of heights and depths, of ascent and descent. Before meeting the beloved, she lay listlessly upon the "drear flat of earth" (27) where she was thrown, and "faint and weak" (12), thought only to "sink" into death (7). Even God's grace, she writes, "Could scarcely lift above the world forlorn / My heavy heart" (25). Where God fails, the beloved succeeds. He has "lifted" her up (27), "snatched" her up (12), and,

> in betwixt the languid ringlets, blown
> A life-breath, till the forehead hopefully
> Shines out again, as all the angels see,
> Before thy saving kiss!
>
> (27)

The infusion of new life leaves her "safe, and strong, and glad" (27).

Since she is saved by being overcome, it is quite appropriate that she should picture the beloved as a conquering soldier:

> Why, conquering
> May prove as lordly and complete a thing
> In lifting upward, as in crushing low!
> And as a vanquished soldier yields his sword
> To one who lifts him from the bloody earth,
> Even so, Belovèd, I at last record,
> Here ends my strife. If *thou* invite me forth,
> I rise above abasement at the word.
>
> (16)

The "I rise" in the final line is significant; she has not passively acquiesced and allowed herself to be lifted; she has been an active participant in her own renewal and has quite willingly been "caught up into love, and taught the whole / Of life in a new rhythm" (7).

While in the opening sonnet the speaker's attraction to the drowsy peace-fulness of death is suggested by slow, hypnotic repetition, in the later poems we frequently become aware of this "new rhythm," a faster and more vigorous rhythm which reflects her growing animation: the pounding of the pulses, of the heart beat, of the blood. Their love leaves their hearts beating together with a double pulse (6), her bosom swells with throbbing new life (27), and her heart beats too fast: "Lay thy hand on it, best one," she invites, "and allow / That no child's foot could run fast as this blood" (34).

The renewed strength and vigor of the speaker after being animated by love are particularly evident in the joyful celebration of sonnet 21, a poem which provides an excellent example of how the vital new rhythm of which she speaks becomes incorporated not only thematically, but also linguistically, into her verse. This sonnet forms a clear contrast with the opening sonnet and reveals just how far she has progressed. Both sonnets rely heavily on repetition to convey the speaker's mood, but while the repetition in sonnet 1 only contributes to the speaker's dreamy passivity, the repetition in sonnet 21 reflects vitality and confidence. No longer content with the "doubtful spirit-voice" that she first heard (21), she now insistently demands repeated proof of the strength of his love:

> Say over again, and yet once over again,
> That thou dost love me. Though the word repeated
> Should seem "a cuckoo-song," as thou dost treat it,
> . . . .
> "Speak once more—thou lovest!" Who can fear
> Too many stars, though each in heaven shall roll,
> Too many flowers, though each shall crown the year?
> Say thou dost love me, love me, love me—toll
> The silver iterance!—only minding, Dear,
> To love me also in silence, with thy soul.
>
> (21)

The jubilant rhythms of "love me, love me, love me" echo both the cuckoo song and the tolling of the bell and strikingly suggest the vigorous new life within her. Instead of dwelling on death and the visionary world of past sorrow, this sonnet rejoices in the natural world, in rebirth, and in the coming of the fresh green Spring.

In the sonnet which follows this joyful affirmation of love and new life, the speaker initiates a significant new twist on the imagery of heights and depths. Apparently taking her own reminder, "love me also in silence, with thy soul," to heart, she seems to begin the sonnet with the intention of now celebrating the spiritual nature of their love:

> When our two souls stand up erect and strong,
> Face to face, silent, drawing nigh and nigher,
> Until the lengthening wings break into fire

> At either curvèd point,—what bitter wrong
> Can the earth do to us, that we should not long
> Be here contented?
>
> (22)

It appears almost inevitable that her attempt to delineate a spiritual love should assume such physical, sensuous proportions. These two souls are hardly ethereal beings; erect and strong, they convey a vigorous sense of a concrete presence. As they draw closer together, gathering momentum is reflected in the building up of clauses and the gradual lengthening of their wings which culminates in the explosive climactic moment when those wings burst into flame. Quite appropriately, considering the new rejoicing in the physical world, the speaker now desires to rise no further; descent replaces ascent as the dominant image:

> In mounting higher,
> The angels would press on us and aspire
> To drop some golden orb of perfect song
> Into our dear, deep silence. Let us stay
> Rather on earth, Belovèd,—where the unfit
> Contrarious moods of men recoil away
> And isolate pure spirits, and permit
> A place to stand and love in for a day,
> With darkness and the death-hour rounding it.
>
> (22)

Her soul, instead of "dreams of death, resumes life's lower range" (23).

The speaker's movement towards a joyful acceptance and celebration of the physical, sensuous world is reflected throughout the sonnets in the manner in which the abstract is repeatedly transformed into the concrete. From the very beginning, when the mystical shape of love proves to be such an undeniably physical force, thoughts, feelings, and gestures continually assume a tangible form. Her love for him, "rising up from breast to brow," manifests itself as a "ruby large enow / To draw men's eyes and prove the inner cost" (12). The ruby, symbol of love, passion, and beauty, and reputed to give health, courage, and happiness, is a most appropriate choice. It becomes a visible sign not only of her love, but also of her new strength and joy.

Similarly, in sonnet 38, the first three kisses that she receives from the beloved materialize as the three elements in an apparent rite of coronation. The first kiss is placed on her fingers: "A ring of amethyst / I could not wear here, plainer to my sight," she claims, and this stone fittingly connects her to the royal purple so frequently associated with the beloved. The second kiss, falling on her hair, is the "chrism of love," the consecrated oil which annoints her before the third, "folded down / In perfect, purple state" upon her lips, presents her with "love's own crown" (38). Notably, in this poem, the speaker herself has come to share in the sensuous appeal that in the early poems is associated with the beloved.

These sonnets are indeed so full of images with such intense tactual appeal, that, upon reaching the end of the sequence, one is left with the impression of having read not about a collection of thoughts, but about a collection of things. This is perhaps partly why the penultimate poem is so disappointing. It is unfortunate that so much attention has been given to "How do I love thee" since it is one of the weaker poems, and, with its insistent listing of abstractions, certainly not representative of the sequence as a whole. Sonnet 44 does, however, provide a fitting conclusion. The thoughts that she has recorded in the preceding poems, the speaker now visualizes as flowers plucked from the garden of her heart. This garden may still be overgrown with "bitter weeds and rue," but she can nevertheless offer him eglantine and ivy, poetry and fidelity, as proof of her love (44). In return for the flowers which he brought to her room, she gives him the metaphorical blossoms which constitute the *Sonnets from the Portuguese*. And the poems themselves provide, of course, the final and most complete example of how the abstract so continually assumes concrete proportions. After their deaths, the speaker regrets, only the spiritual essence of their love will remain:

> Oh, to shoot
> My soul's full meaning into future years,
> That *they* should lend it utterance, and salute
> Love that endures, from Life that disappears!
>
> (41)

This is exactly what she achieves in writing the *Sonnets from the Portuguese*.

The desire to "salute" love, to give expression to the female lyric voice of desire, is Barrett Browning's primary concern in her highly dramatic and richly erotic sonnet sequence. Her personal situation is transformed and exploited for specific dramatic effects, and the self-deprecating emphasis on unworthiness is ultimately a source of strength, not weakness, for both the speaker and the sonnets.

While Barrett Browning appropriates the conventions of the traditional sonnet sequence to accommodate the female lyric voice, she celebrates an active, vital, and sensuous love quite unlike the love typically associated with the traditional form. The devaluation of the female speaker and the glorification of the male beloved aids in a confounding of conventional roles, and the speaker appears not only as passive silent beloved but also as the active subject who gives forceful expression to a vigorous voice of desire. These roles are dramatized primarily with the use of the trope of distance, and the distance imposed between the lovers results in the heightening of erotic satisfaction and in the consummation, when it occurs, being all the more perfect and moving.

Barrett Browning creates a series of images based on the concept of heights, depths, and breadths which is particularly suited both to the female voice and to the concept of gratified, rather than frustrated, desire. Instead of focusing primarily on the visual—which tends to reinforce the idea of distance and separation and to strengthen the notion of an inaccessible beloved—Barrett Browning relies predominantly on the tactual, a form more congenial to the idea of distance surmounted. She soon eliminates both the sense of unattainability typically associated with the object of love and the sense of space typically imposed between lovers. The beloved is exalted precisely because of his vigorous, physical nature and his accessibility; distance is continually imposed between the lovers only to be overcome; and the powerful female lyric voice which expresses and celebrates love in the *Sonnets from the Portuguese* rejoices in the physical and sensuous world, in the joining of the lovers and the intimacy of union.

5

Love and Life: The Expansion of Boundaries in *Aurora Leigh*

In the *Sonnets from the Portuguese*, Barrett Browning focuses exclusively on the growth and celebration of love, and the love that she dramatizes is shown to create a secure and enclosed world of its own into which nothing else intrudes. Like Donne, Barrett Browning imagines a love which "makes one little room an everywhere." The lovers desire to be alone, to maintain their "deep, dear silence," and they find this need for seclusion easily satisfied on earth where

> the unfit
> Contrarious moods of men recoil away
> And isolate pure spirits, and permit
> A place to stand and love in for a day.
>
> (22.9–13)

In *Aurora Leigh* the outside world comes rushing in, Barrett Browning now explores not only the inner spaces of the heart, but also the school rooms, drawing rooms, slums, and brothels of contemporary life. Aurora's desire for love is matched by an equally strong desire to fulfill herself as a poet, and the problems which she must struggle with before she can accept love and her need for love become correspondingly more complex. Reflecting this thematic expansion of boundaries, Barrett Browning moves from the restrictions of the sonnet—which effectively suggests the particular type of love depicted in *Sonnets from the Portuguese* by providing its own form of enclosure—to the freedom offered by a novel in verse which, transgressing the limits of genre, encompasses both the narrative and the lyrical.[1]

The expansion of boundaries tends to lead Barrett Browning away from the particular concern with the female lyric voice of desire—the concern which dominates *Sonnets from the Portuguese*; in *Aurora Leigh* this becomes subordinate to the more general question of the woman as poet. Her other interest with regard to the subject of love, the concern with woman's role in romantic relationships, remains prominent, however, and the expansion of boundaries here allows Barrett Browning to reconsider this question within the larger context of life as a whole rather than within the more narrowly defined limits of the actual relationship. *Aurora Leigh* is more than the story of a woman poet; it is also the story of a woman's growth towards an understanding and acceptance of love, and of her struggle to reconcile the need to fulfill herself in love with the need to fulfill herself as a poet.

The treatment of love in *Aurora Leigh* tends to fall into two overlapping categories: the general question of women and love and the more particular question of Aurora's relationship with Romney. Barrett Browning, who both begins and ends her novel in verse with a celebration of love in Florence, introduces the former question in book 1 with a description of the meeting and marriage of Aurora's parents, and resolves the latter question in book 9 with the reunion of Romney and Aurora, their mutual declaration of love, and their plans for a life together. Significant differences between the types of love celebrated in these two episodes reveal a movement away from the traditional form of love, a form which despite its romantic appeal is male-oriented and tends to define women purely by their roles as wives and mothers, towards a new definition of love which accommodates the needs of each partner in the relationship; they must both be allowed to assume vital active roles, and they must both maintain autonomy as individuals.

Women and Love

Aurora has obviously heard the story of her parents' meeting many times, and the interpretation of the relationship with which we are provided appears to come, indirectly, from the father. This "austere Englishman," concerned primarily with "college-learning, law, and parish talk" (1.67),[2] lives a dull, dry life before meeting his Italian wife; his only avid interest lies in the drains designed by Da Vinci which somewhat ironically first draw him to Italy and love. In Florence, his whole life changes in an instant; a face flashes "like a cymbal on his face . . . / Transfiguring him to music" (1.87–88): he falls in love at first sight. The striking face belongs to one of the "white-veiled rose-crowned maidens" in a religious procession (1.81), and religious terminology is subsequently adopted to describe the experience. Love is a "sacramental gift / With eucharistic meanings" (1.90–91): the outward signs of love are symbolic of an inner spiritual transformation. The most important change effected in Aurora's father is the loosening of emotional restraints; drains forgotten, he is "flooded with a passion unaware" and able to discard conventions, those "chin-bands of the soul" (1.68, 178). Even though his wife's early death leaves him as one "Whom love had unmade from a common man / But not completed to an uncommon man" (1.183–84), the experience of love effects a startling change in his personality.

The father's passionate love for his Italian wife is a source of great strength. It transforms him from a man ruled solely by the intellect, by the traditionally masculine qualities of reason and logic, to a man who combines these traits with the emotional, the traditionally feminine nurturing qualities. He develops a more fully rounded personality by combining the two elements, and when his wife dies, the dual nature of his new character is clearly suggested by his attempt to be both father and mother to Aurora. He wraps his daughter in "his large / Man's doublet" and provides her with an unconventional masculine education (1.726–27); but he also attempts to ensure that she does not entirely miss maternal nurture:

> He left our Florence and made haste to hide
> Himself, his prattling child, and silent grief,
> Among the mountains above Pelago;
> Because unmothered babes, he thought, had need
> Of mother nature more than others use,
> And Pan's white goats, with udders warm and full
> Of mystic contemplations, come to feed
> Poor milkless lips of orphans like his own.
>
> (1.109–16)

Although the father cannot, of course, completely compensate for the mother's absence, he does become a stronger and more complete character because of the experience of love, and, recognizing its importance, he urges Aurora with his dying words: "Love, my child, love, love!" (1.212).

When Aurora refuses Romney's proposal of marriage, it is, significantly, the love of her parents that she recalls; reacting to Romney's reference to her mother, she says:

> You do well to name
> My mother's face. Though far too early, alas,
> God's hand did interpose 'twixt it and me,
> I know so much of love as used to shine
> In that face and another. Just so much;
> No more indeed at all. I have not seen
> So much love since, I pray you pardon me,
> As answers even to make a marriage with
> In this cold land of England.
>
> (2.392–400)

As this passage suggests, the relationship of her parents provides Aurora with the definitive example of love; all other potential love she judges in comparison with this ideal. But Aurora's use of what she knows of her parents' relationship to construct a standard is inevitably problematic. While the romantic tale that she relates certainly suggests intense passion and clearly reveals love's powerful ability to explode conventions, it is nevertheless couched in the traditional terms of romance, full of the conventions of love, and marked by more than a touch of the "Once upon a time." The complex emotions experienced by the father are conveyed in the simplified terms comprehensible to a child, the magic of love is illustrated with the language of the story book romance. Love appears as a highly idealized, completely irrational and spontaneous emotion that is capable of transforming the lover, elevating him far above the needs and concerns of the mundane world. And I use the pronoun "him" intentionally; for all its romantic appeal, the story contains a traditionally male perspective on love. The man is the lover, the woman the rather vague silent and ethereal beloved.

In using the love of her parents as a standard by which all other love is judged, Aurora fails to consider that she is viewing the relationship from her father's—the male—perspective. If she had tried to put herself in her mother's position, it is possible that the romantic tale which she relates might have lost some of its appeal. As the tale clearly shows, love can potentially have quite different effects on men and women.

While the father's passions are associated with strength, the mother's suggest a certain weakness. As a woman, she already possesses an abundance of the emotional traits which the father needed to acquire in order to become a stronger, more complete personality. Her passionate love for her husband and child consequently only intensifies these female qualities, instead of—as in the case of the father—complementing male qualities.[3] The mother is overwhelmed by love, defined entirely by her emotions; and while the father's personality is quite fully realized, we have little sense of the mother as an individual. She begins as the beloved of romance and is then transformed into the ideal mother, a Madonna figure marked by the white of purity and the blue of heavenly love. The self is lost, overwhelmed by the roles. Emotionally strong, she is physically "weak and frail" (1.33); even her death suggests the potentially self-destructive nature of woman's love. A love which nourishes the recipient is shown to possess the ability to debilitate or destroy the giver; the mother "could not bear the joy of giving life, / The mother's rapture slew her" (1.34–35). This is, as Angela Leighton observes, "not a literal death in childbirth which is referred to here, but some vague excess of motherly experience."[4]

Although Aurora desires the kind of passionate love experienced by her parents, she is quite unwilling to assume the conventional female role in a relationship; she silently rebels against the socially approved education in self-repression that the aunt attempts to inflict upon her. This spinster aunt is a masterpiece of tight restraint; her colorless eyes "never, never have forgot themselves / In smiling" (1.283–84), and no words of love come from her cold lips; the hidden tenderness she feels for her brother's child is completely unnoticed by Aurora. The woman's passions are almost totally suppressed; only vehement hatred for Aurora's Italian mother occasionally bursts out in a "strange spasm / Of pain and passion" (1.324–25). Repression speaks even through her tight braids. Aurora's copious curls are soon similarly plaited as the aunt sets about weeding out all her Italian nonsense and instructing the girl in the womanly art of self-suppression; she intends to transform Aurora into the "womanly" woman (1.443), one of the Englishwomen who are "models to the universe" (1.446). Dutiful, self-effacing, and devoid of personal ambition, these paragons are concerned only to tend to their families, to soothe their husbands, stroking their "temples cool / With healthy touches" (2.647–48). Aurora's scathing commentary on the training involved in producing this almost mythic creature neatly lights upon the contradictions inherent in an ideology which first assigns women spiritual superiority and inordinate virtue and then condemns them to exert their "Potential faculty in everything / Of abdicating power in it" (1.441–42). Everything that Aurora learns about love and marriage seems to suggest that the only role available to women in romantic relationships necessarily involves a selfless renunciation of all personal desire and personal ambition, and a total dedication to the needs of others.

The adult Aurora's ambivalence towards women and love is strikingly prefigured in the young Aurora's response to her mother's death portrait. Paradoxically, the woman who is depicted in this portrait is a far more vital and vigorous figure than the rose-crowned maiden or angelic mother she was when alive. The "swan-like supernatural white life" (1.139) springs to life in the flickering firelight and reveals a dead white face rising above a body of disturbing power, a body no longer associated with ethereal blues and innocuous whites but dressed in violent red stiff silk that is quite unable to keep the straining white flesh from "breaking out of bounds" (1.142).

There is a marked resemblance between this portrait and Aurora's later description of the pointedly fleshy and lascivious Lady Waldemar, who is distinguished by the same strikingly contrasted reds and whites. With a curious mixture of admiration, envy, and disgust, Aurora records:

> How they told,
> Those alabaster shoulders and bare breasts,
> On which the pearls, drowned out of sight in milk,
> Were lost, excepting for the ruby clasp!
> They split the amaranth velvet bodice down
> To the waist or nearly, with the audacious press
> Of full-breathed beauty. If the heart within
> Were half as white!—but, if it were, perhaps

> The breast were closer covered and the sight
> Less aspectable by half, too.
>
> (5.619–27)

The similarity in the images seems to suggest a potentially vigorous and active sexuality in the two women—both the alive and the dead. The mother is no longer subsumed or overwhelmed but becomes, by displaying the stark contrast of red and white, life and death, the embodiment of the elemental female; she consequently provides an appropriate canvas on which Aurora can impose her various views of women.

As Aurora grows, she mixes everything she hears, reads, or dreams about women with her mother's face, and this face assumes, by turns, the characteristics of numerous archetypal and fragmented images of women:

> Ghost, fiend, and angel, fairy, witch, and sprite,
> A dauntless Muse who eyes a dreadful Fate,
> A loving Psyche who loses sight of Love,
> A still Medusa with mild milky brows
> All curdled and all clothed upon with snakes
> Whose slime falls fast as sweat will; or anon
> Our Lady of the Passion, stabbed with swords
> Where the Babe sucked; or Lamia in her first
> Moonlighted pallor, ere she shrunk and blinked
> And shuddering wriggled down to the unclean.
>
> (1.154–63)

Gazing upon the mother "half in terror, half / In adoration" (1.137–38), Aurora begins to view women as a bunch of moral and sexual splinters or "incoherencies" (1.171)—not as something she identifies with, but as something to be viewed and analyzed from a distance.

Aurora's desire to repress the feminine and identify with the masculine is suggestively conveyed by her responses to yet another attempt at a visual representation of woman: Vincent Carrington's two sketches of Danae. The implications of the red and white in the death portrait are here split and reflected in a simplified form by Carrington's attempt to represent two types of female love. The first Danae, as Carrington describes her to Aurora, is blatantly erotic; driven by sexual desire and aggressively demanding fulfillment, she almost springs off the page:

> A tiptoe Danae, overbold and hot,
> Both arms a-flame to meet her wishing Jove
> Halfway, and burn him faster down; the face

> And breasts upturned and straining, the loose locks
> All glowing with the anticipated gold.
>
> (3.122–26)

The second Danae, in contrast, is passively lost in the ecstasy of love:

> She lies here—flat upon her prison floor,
> The long hair swathed about her to the heel
> Like wet seaweed. You dimly see her through
> The glittering haze of the prodigious rain,
> Half blotted out of nature by a love
> As heavy as fate.
>
> (3.128–33)

Although the first Danae displays the most obvious sexual appeal, it is nevertheless the second, the woman whose self is lost, "Half blotted out" by love, that Carrington depicts with the images of snaky slithering wetness and streaming hair repeatedly used by characters in *Aurora Leigh* to suggest erotic awareness. And indeed, Carrington believes the second sketch preferable, finding more passion in woman's self-abnegation than in woman's aggression.

Aurora's instinctive reaction to Carrington's declared preference would suggest that initially she identifies with the female perspective—the woman depicted rather than the man who sketches. Recognizing in Carrington that conventional view of women which originally led her to reject the female role, she dryly observes "Surely. Self is put away, / And calm with abdication. She is Jove, / And no more Danae—greater thus" (3.135–37). Immediately, however, Aurora rejects this implicit female perspective by assuming the role of artist, a role which allows her to move away from painful identification with the woman as object:

> Perhaps
> The painter symbolizes unaware
> Two states of the recipient artist-soul,
> One, forward, personal, wanting reverence,
> Because aspiring only. We'll be calm,
> And know that, when indeed our Joves come down,
> We all turn stiller than we have ever been.
>
> (3.137–43)

This presentation of Aurora's reactions to the two Danaes forms an interesting contrast with her later association of herself with Io. When Aurora envisions herself as the object of Jove's attentions, she makes a determined effort to view the story from an artistic, rather than an amorous perspective. Referring to her lifelong attempt to write "truth," she claims:

> I, Aurora, still
> Have felt it hound me through the wastes of life
> As Jove did Io; and until that Hand
> Shall overtake me wholly and on my head
> Lay down its large unfluctuating peace,
> The feverish gad-fly pricks me up and down.
>
> (7.828–33)

This interpretation of the myth is significantly confused. Io is actually hounded not by Jove, but by the gad-fly sent by Hera. Jove finally restores her to human form with a simple touch of the hand, and she subsequently gives birth to Epaphus, "the touch." Aurora appears to conflate truth with both Jove and the gad-fly, and by focusing on Jove as pursuer, and upon that moment when Io is transformed, she actually emphasizes the erotic nature of the myth. Barrett Browning could conceivably have had in mind Correggio's highly erotic painting of the hand laid on a very human and sensual Io. And soon after this, Aurora herself recognizes the true focus of her desires:

> Is it so?
> When Jove's hand meets us with composing touch,
> And when at last we are hushed and satisfied,
> Then Io does not call it truth, but love?
>
> (7.894–97)

Barrett Browning's characterization of Marian and Lady Waldemar provides another example of the division of woman's love into two opposing types. These women are sometimes considered to be unbelievable stereotypes, lifeless "Keepsake lithographs of the Poor but Virtuous Maiden and the Wicked Lady of Quality."[5] To the extent that this is true, it is also necessary, and it is more a reflection of the manner in which Aurora views the women than of Barrett Browning's failure to infuse her characters with life.[6] Marian and Lady Waldemar provide the familiar split between flesh and spirit shown in such other paired characters as Hardy's Sue and Arabella, and Brontë's St. John and Rochester. The common ploy is varied, however, and one woman finds her choice embodied in two other women. These women appear as aspects of Aurora herself, and she must find her way between the merely spiritual and the merely sensual to a love which combines the two.

In her presentation of Marian, Barrett Browning could conceivably be recollecting Mary Wollstonecraft's complaint about "Gentleness, docility, and a spaniel-like affection" being "consistently recommended as the cardinal virtues of the sex."[7] Marian, with her "infantile smile," "milky little teeth," and "spaniel head" (3.823, 822; 9.276), who upon Romney's arrival waits "doglike . . . / Most passionately patient . . . / A-tremble for her turn of greeting words"

(4.281–83), appears to have all these "virtues." And she adores Romney: "I'd rather far be trodden by his foot / Than lie in a great queen's bosom" (4.217–18), Marian declares—and the reader cannot doubt it.

It is hardly surprising that while contemporary reviewers felt that Aurora was "not a genuine woman" and found the "high-souled female with 'a mission' to be a terrible companion in a journey of twelve thousand lines," they heartily approved of the unselfish and feminine Marian.[8] Aurora's approbation, however, is not so easily comprehended. Marian does, after all, embody the self-effacing woman that Aurora refuses to become. The numerous images of timid animals and delicate flowers which Aurora uses to describe Marian perhaps provide a clue to her approval of Romney's choice for a wife. When Romney calls Aurora "my flower" (2.828), she thoroughly resents the implication that women are fragile and weak; "certain flowers," she snaps, "grow near as deep as trees" (2.848). But Aurora in turn associates Marian with delicate flowers, rustling birds, and wandering deer. Her choice of such images seems to be a reflection of her identification with the masculine perspective. Aurora reveals the same mixture of condescension and adulation in her response to Marian as Romney once showed towards her.

Aurora's views on the nature of woman's love seem to be confirmed by Marian's adoration of Romney. "This perhaps was love," she considers, "To have its hands too full of gifts to give, / For putting out a hand to take a gift" (4.176–78). Barrett Browning, however, clearly shows that there are flaws in both Marian and the love she offers Romney. From Aurora's description of Marian, the reader can detect a lack of strength and a certain incompleteness in the girl's character:

> Nowise beautiful
> Was Marian Erle. She was not white nor brown,
> But could look either, like a mist that changed
> According to being shone on more or less:
> The hair, too, ran its opulence of curls
> In doubt 'twixt dark and bright, nor left you clear
> To name the colour.
>
> (3.809–15)

There is no sense of a strong identity here; Marian appears as an ethereal creature who even derives her appearance from her surroundings.

It is questionable whether Marian's feelings for Romney provide an adequate basis for a relationship. She intends to be both handmaid and wife, to "serve tenderly, and love obediently" (4.227–29). All she desires is the opportunity to give of herself; her love is a "simple fealty on one side, / A mere religion,—right to give, is all" (4.193–94). When Aurora asks, "He loves you, Marian?" (4.169), the puzzled response suggests that Marian has not even considered being loved in return. Her willingness to be consumed entirely in the Western equivalent of suttee is not likely to provoke unqualified admiration in the modern reader (4.195–202).

While Marian represents a pure, selfless, and highly spiritual love, Lady Waldemar represents a calculating sexual love. Aurora dislikes the woman on their first meeting, long before she becomes aware of the lengths to which Lady Waldemar is prepared to go in her overwhelming desire for Romney. While part of Aurora's dislike can be attributed to her disapproval of Lady Waldemar's flippant willingness to "love and lie" (3.708), the vehemence of her obvious revulsion suggests her response is more complicated than this: Aurora also appears to be repelled by the woman because she freely and aggressively expresses sexual desire.

Lady Waldemar, aptly labeled an "eye-trap" (5.853), carefully sets herself up as a sexual object, and prominently displays her charms. All her dealings with others are conducted on a sensual level; she even initially attempts a type of seduction on Aurora, skillfully using her melting eyes, swinging her curls, and continually clasping Aurora's hands. Lady Waldemar's feelings for Romney are conveyed in the traditional language of love—melancholy but suffused with the earthy accents of sexual passion; "You eat of love," she tells Aurora,

> And do as vile a thing as if you ate
> Of garlic—which, whatever else you eat,
> Tastes uniformly acrid, till your peach
> Reminds you of your onion. Am I coarse?
> Well, love's coarse, nature's coarse—ah, there's the rub.
> We fair fine ladies, who park out our lives
> From common sheep-paths, cannot help the crows
> From flying over,—we're as natural still
> As Blowsalinda. . . .
>   We catch love,
> And other fevers, in the vulgar way.
>
>   (3.450–66)

The reviewers agreed with Lady Waldemar's self-estimation and found her not only coarse but revolting. They could not understand why her conversation had to be "so flavoured with allusions to garlic."[9]

Aurora barely conceals her own disgust. With a fastidiousness reminiscent of her father's early concern with hygiene, she coldly begins to speak of worthiness and cleanliness: "Whoever loves him," she priggishly exhorts,

> let her not excuse
> But cleanse herself, that, loving such a man,

> She may not do it with such unworthy love
> He cannot stoop and take it.
>
> (3.481–84)

Such an openly lusty love as Lady Waldemar's only disgusts Aurora. She declares such feelings barely worthy of the name of love. Consequently, she is soon distorting the very nature of Lady Waldemar's passion; "if she loves at last," Aurora decides, "Her love's a re-adjustment of self-love, / No more,—a need felt of another's use / To her one advantage" (4.521–23). This is not quite a fair assessment; there is no evidence that Lady Waldemar's love is as superficial as Aurora wishes to believe. Her feelings for Romney are perhaps the most sincere element of her character.

Aurora's need to transform sexual passion into selfish desire is telling; while she is able to decline the role of the self-effacing woman represented by Marian, she finds that a complete rejection of her female nature is not so simple. Lady Waldemar, no saint but a self-proclaimed "mere woman" (3.490), is therefore more difficult for Aurora to deal with. The natural passions that Lady Waldemar so openly expresses, Aurora cannot simply refuse to experience; the masculine stance that she adopts can never be more than a stance, and her passions cannot be ignored. Lady Waldemar consequently becomes an unpleasant reminder to Aurora of what she is unsuccessfully trying to repress. While Aurora's reading of Lady Waldemar is distorted and her understanding of herself limited, Lady Waldemar can read *her* like a well-perused book. After one conversation with the woman, Aurora is left pained and bewildered by Lady Waldemar's ability to pierce her "steel-mail" (5.1044) with the needle of spite:

> What vexes, after all,
> Is just that such as she, with such as I,
> Knows how to vex. Sweet heaven, she takes me up
> As if she had fingered me and dog-eared me
> And spelled me by the fireside half a life!
>
> (5.1051–55)

Both women have the same desires, but only Lady Waldemar openly recognizes them.

While Barrett Browning certainly approves of a woman with a masculine intellect, she does not believe it either possible or desirable for a woman to reject what is essentially female in her nature.[10] In "To George Sand. A Recognition" (1844), she calls Sand's attempt to reject the female a "vain denial": "Thy woman's hair, my sister, all unshorn / Floats back dishevelled strength in agony, / Disproving thy man's name" (2.239). Female emotion, female passion, is here seen as a strength by Barrett Browning, and not, as Aurora initially views it, as a weakness.[11] The success and vitality of Sand's work are to a great extent dependent on the "woman-heart" (2.239) which so clearly beats within it. Not surprisingly, Aurora's problems are only increased by her attempt to repress the "mere woman" in her, to deny her desire and need for love.

Consequently, I cannot agree that Aurora's relationship with Marian is as satisfying as many critics claim. For Nina Auerbach, "*Aurora Leigh* celebrates the choric power of female community; its triumphant achievement is not Aurora's marriage to the diminished Romney, but her union with the victimized seamstress Marian Erle."[12] Such an interpretation, I believe, forces a modern feminist perspective on the poem that the text simply cannot support. Aurora is actually quite unable to find satisfaction in her relationship with Marian. "I am lonely in the world / And thou art lonely" she says (7.120–21), and she attempts to overcome this loneliness by creating a new family circle. But during all the time that they are in Italy together prior to Romney's arrival, there are only two brief references to Marian and the child—and both tend to suggest less a sense of community than Aurora's continuing sense of isolation. The picture of Marian happily absorbed by her child in the garden below while Aurora sits alone upon the terrace of her tower only suggests a barrier between the two women, while references to the laughter and kisses of the child leave Aurora struggling unsuccessfully to convince herself "Surely I should be glad," and "I should certainly be glad" (7.952, 957). After the initial ardent protestations of sisterhood, the relationship tends to fizzle away. While we might like to think Barrett Browning capable of envisioning a relationship between two women as completely satisfying, the text cannot support such a supposition.

Marian is, however, responsible for Aurora's eventual ability to break through the barriers which she has erected. The relationship prompts Aurora to express emotion and respond as a woman. When Aurora first assumes Marian has been seduced, she forces herself to be cold and judgmental; characteristically, she talks of worthiness and cleanliness. The child is "well enough," she grudgingly admits:

> If his mother's palms are clean
> They need be glad of course in clasping such;
> But if not, I would rather lay my hand,
> Were I she, on God's brazen altar-bars
> Red-hot with burning sacrificial lambs,
> Than touch the sacred curls of such a child.
>
> (6.617–23)

But Marian refuses to accept the conventional role of fallen woman, and she speaks out in her own defense. Hearing that Marian was raped, not seduced, Aurora radically revises her attitude; finally she responds with "woman's passion" (6.779), as one woman to another. Marian is as innocent now, she claims, as she was before. Aurora is beginning to mature, to integrate the various guises of women and to accept her own female nature.

This release of "woman's passion" also allows Aurora's feelings for Romney to surface, and, fearing that she has lost him to Lady Waldemar, she punctuates the remainder of Marian's tale with her own tormenting thoughts—"Is it time / For church now," she wonders, and "Perhaps he's sliding now the ring / Upon that woman's finger" (6.1102–3, 1119–20). Marian's importance inevitably diminishes; as Aurora becomes more aware of her own needs, she can only become more aware of the emptiness of her life without Romney. Marian's tale over, Aurora concludes:

> It is strange,
> To-day while Marian told her story like
> To absorb most listeners, how I listened chief
> To a voice not hers, . . .
> . . . but one that mixed with mine
> Long years ago among the garden-trees,
> And said to *me*, to *me* too, "Be my wife."
>
> (7.174–80)

Romney, the Sea-King

Time has, of course, clearly softened Aurora's memories of that June day when Romney proposed. She was not exactly moved in quite the same way then as she is now in recollection. Before Romney makes his rather clumsy and prosaic proposal, Aurora does indeed sense his love for her, but that proposal soon changes her opinion of his "love-making" quite radically.

The reader is presented with two views of the early Romney, and Aurora's portrayal of her cousin as cold, unfeeling, and overly concerned with logic and statistics is somewhat at odds with her memories of the man who sometimes seemed to sigh in her direction (1.530), who leads her away from the music and needle work that she despises into the garden to "see in that south angle of the house / The figs grow black as if by a Tuscan rock" (1.535–36). Sometimes, she remembers, "He would have saved me utterly, it seemed, / He stood and looked so" (1.541–42). When Romney looks at her so gently and speaks with "such a voice" (2.771), he reveals his love in the conventional ways which Aurora can understand. His actions seem to embody some of the magical love found in the parents' relationship. The actual proposal, however, convinces Aurora that she has quite misunderstood his feelings for her.

Romney finds Aurora's intellectual ambitions occasionally endearing, frequently irritating, and constantly amusing. His own obsessive concern with his philanthropical schemes completely blinds him to the importance of poetry to

Aurora, and his conventional views of woman's role result in an inability to see Aurora as an individual with her own needs and desires; he sees women defined only by their roles in love relationships, as "doating mothers, and perfect wives, / Sublime Madonnas, and enduring saints" (2.22–23). They are capable of personal, passionate, and selfless love, he believes, but not of universal compassion or the general understanding necessary for the creation of art. "We get no Christ from you," he smugly announces, "and verily / We shall not get a poet" (2.223–25). As Aurora indignantly responds with a defense of her right to pursue her own vocation, an ideological discussion on art and service begins to dominate the scene. Romney condescendingly dismisses Aurora's dreams of achieving artistic success and asks her to marry him and devote herself to his philanthropical schemes. Aurora rejects his limited views of women's role, refuses his proposal, and claims that she has her own work to do. The reader must surely sympathize with the exasperated reviewer who labeled Romney a "decided noodle."[13] He is quite unable to see Aurora as an individual with personal needs, and his declaration of love is almost lost in a torrent of words as he eagerly seeks to inspire Aurora with his own zeal for reform.

In comparison with the father's passionate, irrational, and spontaneous love, Romney's feelings are certainly disappointingly dull and prosaic. But to dismiss this as a "loveless proposal of marriage" is surely wrong.[14] As Romney's desperate attempts at clarification—"you translate me ill" and "read me now a little plainer" (2.369, 820)—suggest, Aurora does not see the love that he struggles to convey. This does not mean, however, that the love does not exist.[15] Aurora is not always the most reliable of narrators; she is as obsessed with her own plans as Romney is with his, and while despising those women who "Will sometimes only hear the first word, love, / And catch up with it any kind of work, / Indifferent, so that dear love go with it" (2.445–47), she falls into the opposite trap. From the very beginning of their exchange, Aurora is defensive; she has been caught in an embarrassing situation, crowning herself as poet with a wreath of ivy. Romney's scorn for her vocation makes an unpromising situation even worse; reacting violently to this scorn, the indignant Aurora is oblivious to his declaration of love. When he pleads with her: "Place your fecund heart / In mine and let us blossom for the world / That wants love's color in the grey of time" (2.375–77), Aurora only hears:

> I have some worthy work for thee below.
> Come, sweep my barns and keep my hospitals,
> And I will pay thee with a current coin
> Which men give women.
>
> (2.538–41)

An overemphasis on ideology prevents one from clearly articulating and the other from interpreting. Gestures and silences become more reliable guides to feelings than words, but Romney and Aurora are poor readers of these; ironically, only the spinster aunt can translate the "weather signs of love" (2.691).

Even if Romney had displayed the type of passionate love desired by Aurora, however, this would not have resolved all the obstacles to their union. The manner in which Aurora envisions the alternative scene is telling:

> If he had loved,
> Ay, loved me, with that retributive face,...
> I might have been a common woman now
> And happier, less known and less left alone,
> Perhaps a better woman after all,
> With chubby children hanging on my neck
> To keep me low and wise.
>
> (2.511–17)

For Aurora, this passive role is really quite unacceptable; the desire for love consequently begins to appear as no more than a weakness that must be overcome, a dangerous yearning to "lose ourselves / And melt like white pearls in another's wine" (5.1078–79). The "female" side of her personality which causes her to long for fulfillment in love is seen as inseparable from what is weak, personal, and emotional, and is contemptuously dismissed as the "poor conscious trouble of blood / That's called the woman merely" (7.231–32).

Rejecting any attempt to treat her as if she were a "mere" woman, Aurora insists upon being spoken to "man to man" (5.811). If she can repress the feminine, she believes, she will be incapable of love; and so: "I cannot love," she tells Lord Howe, "I only find / The rhyme for love,—and that's not love, my lord" (5.895–96).

Looking back on her refusal of Romney's proposal, Aurora firmly declares:

> I attest
> The conscious skies and all their daily suns,
> I think I loved him not,—nor then, nor since,
> Nor ever.
>
> (2.711–14)

The uncertain "I think" in the midst of such dogmatic assertions is revealing. Repression is clearly not the answer to Aurora's problem.

Barrett Browning repeatedly provides us with evidence of Aurora's initially unconscious love. The sudden blush on her face when her aunt declares: "I am not old for nothing; I can tell / The weather signs of love: you love this man" (2.690–91) clearly confirms that the aunt is right. And Aurora's behavior on the following occasions when she meets Romney movingly conveys the extent of her self-deception. When the aunt's will had been read, Aurora remembers:

> We rose up in a silence almost hard,
> And looked at one another. Then I said,
> "Farewell, my cousin." But he touched, just touched
> My hatstrings, tied for going (at the door
> The carriage stood to take me), and said low,
> His voice a little unsteady through his smile,
> "Siste, viator."
>
> (2.968–74)

As soon as they begin to talk, of course, Aurora gets angry, and the moment is lost. But the very fact that Aurora remembers that simple gesture and dwells upon it—"But he touched, just touched"—suggests that this was a highly charged emotional moment for her. After this meeting,

> we let go hands, my cousin and I,
> And in between us rushed the torrent-world
> To blanch our faces like divided rocks,
> And bar for ever mutual sight and touch
> Except through whirl of spray and all that roar.
>
> (2.1244–48)

Aurora's love for Romney is usually suggested by references to silences and distances between them; it is in such references that her longing can most poignantly be found. Their next parting—after a meeting at Marian's—is described in similar terms. During their "strange and melancholy walk" when Romney accompanies her home (4.393), Aurora recalls, "The act, the presence, my hand upon his arm, / His voice in my ear, and mine to my own sense, / Appeared unnatural" (4.396–98). Their closeness seems to bring danger:

> We talked on fast, while every common word
> Seemed tangled with the thunder at one end,
> And ready to pull down upon our head
> A terror out of sight. And yet to pause
> Were surelier mortal: we tore greedily up
> All silence, all the innocent breathing-points.
>
> (4.408–13)

That "thunder," their emotions, continually threatens to burst out.

While Barrett Browning continually suggests, through her depiction of Aurora, that a woman without love is incomplete, she also shows, through her depiction of Marian, that such incompleteness is preferable to accepting a loveless or imperfect marriage. According to Barrett Browning, "Marian had to be dragged through the uttermost debasement of circumstances to arrive at the sentiment of personal dignity" (EBB 2.242).

When Marian emerges in the final scene to reject Romney's final offer of marriage, she is in many ways a cold and unearthly figure:

> She stood there, still and pallid as a saint
> Dilated, like a saint in ecstasy,
> As if the floating moonlight interposed
> Betwixt her foot and the earth, and raised her up
> To float upon it.
>
> (9.187–91)

But it is at this moment that Aurora first sees that "Marian Erle was beautiful" (9.186), and this new beauty results from a new dignity. There is now pride and authority in Marian's voice, and when Aurora uses the old imagery of wild animals to describe her, there is a significant change. Marian is no longer a timid woodland creature; she may escape from Romney's embrace like a "leaping fawn," but she then stands before him with a "staglike majesty / Of soft, serene defiance" (9.288–91). In a speech somewhat reminiscent of Jane Eyre's "I care for myself," Marian reveals the cause of her new self-respect:

> I, who felt myself unworthy once
> Of virtuous Romney and his high-born race,
> Have come to learn,—a woman, poor or rich,
> Despised or honoured, is a human soul,
> And what her soul is, that she is herself,
> Although she should be spit upon of men.
>
> (9.326–31)

Marian is unwilling to give herself to a loveless marriage with Romney; she feels clean and strong as Marian Erle. The manner in which she describes her previous feelings for Romney clearly suggests her recognition that such self-effacement did not constitute love, but worship; she only thought, she admits,

> To be your slave, your help, you toy, your tool.
> To be your love...I never thought of that:
> To give you love...still less. I gave you love?
> I think I did not give you anything;
> I was but only yours—upon my knees,
> All yours, in soul and body, in head and heart,
> A creature you had taken from the ground

> Still crumbling through your fingers to your feet
> To join the dust she came from.
>
> (9.370–78)

There is indeed, as Barrett Browning said, a new personal dignity in Marian's awareness that she has her own worth and cannot simply be the tool or toy of another.

But while Marian displays a certain self-sufficiency in her detachment from Romney, Aurora remains incomplete and unfulfilled; her success as a poet does not compensate for the dreariness of her life alone: "If this then be success, 'tis dismaller / Than any failure" (5.433–34). The belief that she has lost Romney to Lady Waldemar prompts Aurora to return to Italy, fleeing from the clanking marriage bells that seem to pursue her, and also, apparently, fleeing from mature sexuality. Barrett Browning's description of the train journey renders a powerful sense of Aurora's obsession; the belfry bells which she imagines, "fifty bells / Of naked iron, mad with merriment" (7.401–2), violently merge with the rhythms of the train, and the clangor sends Aurora, shrieking, into a swoon.

Aurora returns to her homeland like a child seeking the comforts of the mother, yearning towards the hills that she has heard crying to her throughout her life:

> And now I come, my Italy,
> My own hills! Are you 'ware of me, my hills,
> The urgency and yearning of my soul,
> As sleeping mothers feel the sucking babe
> And smile?
>
> (5.1266–71)

As Sandra Gilbert observes, Italy is presented in *Aurora Leigh* as both "a nurturing mother—a land that feeds" and an "impassioned sister—a land that feels."[16] Aurora's early descriptions of her homeland capture both the maternal and the sensual elements. She remembers "headlong leaps / Of waters, that cry out for joy or fear / In leaping through the palpitating pines" (1.617–19) and "multitudinous mountains, sitting in / The magic circle, with the mutual touch / Electric, panting from their full deep hearts" (1.622–24). In England, the fatherland, nature is conversely tamed and trimmed:

> All the fields
> Are tied up fast with hedges, nosegay-like;
> The hills are crumpled plains, the plains parterres,
> The trees, round, woolly, ready to be clipped,
> And if you seek for any wilderness
> You find, at best, a park.
>
> (1.629–34)

Here, Aurora can find neither maternal nor sensual love.

But while Aurora returns to Italy seeking the "nurturing mother," it is primarily the "impassioned sister" that she encounters. She is unable to recreate the innocent times of childhood; her old "Tuscan pleasures" are "worn and spoiled" (7.1041), and a visit to her old mountain home leaves her aware that she has come back "to an empty nest, / Which every bird's too wise for" (7.1109–10). All trace of her previous life has been erased. She longs for a "drop of dew / To cool this heat,—a drop of the early dew, / The irrecoverable child-innocence" (7.1102–4); but flight from her mature passions is no longer possible. The vibrant green land of her youth is now fiery red and stifling.

Aurora's growing frustration and unhappiness in Italy are skillfully captured in images of heat and tedium. Although she tries to convince herself that she is happy, that her native air sits upon her easily (7.928–29), the setting becomes increasingly oppressive. The "hot sick air" weighs upon her (7.994), and the growing heat and noises of the seething land become a reflection of her building passion and the vexing heart beat which threatens to overwhelm her. Dissatisfied with her "ragged, narrow life" (7.919), Aurora wanders through the streets like "a restless ghost" (7.1161), only to be faced with the sight of

> Each lovely lady close to a cavalier
> Who holds her dear fan while she feeds her smile
> On meditative spoonfuls of vanille
> And listens to his hot-breathed vows of love
> Enough to thaw her cream and scorch his beard.
>
> (7.1182–86)

The highly sensual nature of this provocative description is telling. Although Aurora can never admit that Lady Waldemar is more than a "wind from hell" (3.284), she does begin to experience the same driving passions as the woman that she scorns. As Lady Waldemar airily claims "we're as natural . . . as Blowsa-linda" (3.458–59), so Aurora recognizes "we are all slaves to nature" (7.967); as all the love-sick Lady Waldemar's cards "Turned up but Romney Leigh" (3.470), so Romney's name becomes for Aurora "too like a tune that runs / I'the head" (7.960–61).

Still attempting to fight her desires, Aurora scorns herself for wanting "the beast's part now" and "tiring of the angels" (7.1005–6); the flesh she sees as a "soaked / And sucking vesture" which threatens to drag her down into "the melancholy Deep" (7.1031–33). The sea image recalls Aurora's description of her aunt's attempt to drain her of her Italian passions; she became, she writes:

> Like sea-weed on the rocks, and suffering her
> To prick me to a pattern with her pin,
> Fibre from fibre, delicate leaf from leaf
> And dry out from my drowned anatomy
> The last sea-salt left in me.

(1.380–84)

Images of water, flooding, and drowning are used throughout *Aurora Leigh* to suggest passion or the abandonment of the self to passion—the father, for example, is flooded unaware, and Carrington's second Danae is swathed with wet seaweed. Repressing her desire, preferring to walk the waves (7.1034), Aurora becomes "withered life" (7.1105); she completes the process begun by the aunt herself.

Barbara Gelpi has noted that Aurora's "final reconciliation with her womanhood comes in a Florentine church."[17] In this scene, Aurora begins as a detached observer. Considering the faces of the supplicants who look most in need—women, she records with contempt—Aurora once more fails to identify with the women she sees and instead transforms them into objects of her art; spinning tales to fit each face, she ironically deflates their prayers and their obvious loneliness. Feeling infinitely superior, she concedes that God may hear their prayers since "He heareth the young ravens cry / And yet they cry for carrion" (7.1262–63). Aurora is never quite as insufferable as at this moment. Fortunately, she regains the reader's sympathy by making the important transition from observer to participant. Recognizing her fellowship with the women she scorns, she admits that she too is "foolish in desire / Like other creatures craving offal-food," and kneeling, she prays for God to ignore her words and "only listen to the run and beat / Of this poor, passionate, helpless blood" (7.1267–71). Although "offal-food" still suggests a less than healthy attitude towards her own desires, Aurora certainly shows much progress.

While she has previously believed the woman's loss of self inevitably to result from giving in to love, Aurora now sees that it may also be caused by the absence of love. Sitting alone during the gloomy nights, she begins to feel

> Most like some passive broken lump of salt,
> Dropped in by chance to a bowl of oenomel,
> To spoil the drink a little and lose itself,
> Dissolving slowly, slowly, until lost.

(7.1308–11)

And as Aurora withers for lack of love, her creativity withers too: "At such times, ended seemed my trade of verse," she claims, "I did not write, nor read, nor even think" (8.1302, 1306). We are not offered a theory of sublimation in which frustrated desire is fruitfully channeled into artistic production, but rather a theory of a fulfilled life leading to a fulfilled art.

The oenomel image, a distorted variation on the images of flooding and drowning, aptly leads into the climactic moment when Aurora watches from her tower as the city becomes flooded by the evening shadows "like some drowned city in some enchanted sea" (8.38) and feels drawn,

> With passionate desire, to leap and plunge,
> And find a sea-king with a voice of waves,
> And treacherous soft eyes, and slippery locks
> You cannot kiss but you shall bring away
> Their salt upon your lips.
>
> (8.40–44)

The sea-king is clearly envisioned in the image of Romney—whose marriage proposal had seemed to belie the love which she sensed in his soft looks and tender voice. As Aurora imagines that she has plunged into the sea, abandoned herself to desire, Romney makes his well-timed entrance.

There are a number of problems with the conclusion of *Aurora Leigh*, partly because, as a contemporary reviewer noted, "we see the agony more fully than the remedy."[18] One passage in Aurora's final declaration of love is particularly troublesome:

> I would not be a woman like the rest,
> A simple woman who believes in love
> And owns the right of love because she loves,
> And, hearing she's beloved, is satisfied
> With what contents God: I must analyse,
> Confront, and question; just as if a fly
> Refused to warm itself in any sun
> Till such was *in Leone:* I must fret,
> Forsooth, because the month was only May,
> Be faithless of the kind of proffered love,
> And captious, lest it miss my dignity,
> And scornful, that my lover sought a wife
> To use.
>
> (9.660–72)

Apart from the obvious fact that Aurora did not previously recognize that she *was* loved, this passage is disturbing since it appears to contradict some of the primary points made in *Aurora Leigh*. First, Barrett Browning has spent much of the previous eight books convincing the reader that while Aurora was wrong in much, she was right in refusing to accept the type of relationship offered by Romney, a relationship in which the woman's identity would be completely subsumed. In this passage, however, Aurora appears to be suggesting that she should have accepted Romney when he first proposed.

Furthermore, as Kathleen Blake points out, "If she had not analyzed, confronted, and questioned, and been complicated enough to distrust love, Romney would never have come around to see that women can produce great poems, because she would not have produced one."[19] Although art and love *seem* irreconcilable, Barrett Browning has not suggested that Aurora should have abandoned her art and been satisfied with love; she has, on the contrary, shown one way in which the two can be reconciled. As Aurora observes in her speech on those who "prate of woman's rights, / Of woman's mission, woman's function" (8.819–20), if women work towards demonstrating their abilities, then

> there's no need to speak;
> The universe shall henceforth speak for you,
> And witness, "She who did this thing was born
> To do it—claims her license in her work."
> And so with more works. Whoso cures the plague,
> Though twice a woman, shall be called a leech:
> Who rights a land's finances is excused
> For touching coppers, though her hands be white.
>
> (8.838–45)

The solution may be, in practice, somewhat over-simplified, but this is never ntheless the way in which Aurora has reconciled art and love: her book proves her abilities to Romney, and he is consequently able to form a relationship in which her rights as a poet, as an individual, are honored.

Although life without love has become intolerable for Aurora, even after she becomes aware that Romney loves her, is free to marry her, and has recognized the importance of her work, she is still unable to declare her own love until she knows that Romney is blind. It is difficult to find a satisfactory reason for the necessity of blinding Romney, and Barrett Browning's explanation—"He had to be blinded, observe, to be made to see...I am sorry, but indeed it seemed necessary" (EBB 2.242)—is, as Barbara Gelpi complains, "not a particularly enlightening answer, since Aurora too comes to 'see' herself and others very much better in the course of the poem, but is physically unscathed in the process."[20]

In her discussion of the recurrent motif of the blinded or disfigured hero in nineteenth-century women's fiction, Elaine Showalter concludes that it "does seem to show outright hostility, if not castration wishes, towards men." She also adds, however, that "these humiliations of the hero are not merely punitive"; women novelists believed that "a limited experience of dependency, frustration, and powerlessness—in short, of womanhood—was a healthy and instructive one for the hero."[21] This final point seems particularly relevant to the blinding of the hero in *Aurora Leigh*. Conjecture about the possibility of hostility or castration wishes being present in Barrett Browning's decision to blind her hero seems relatively futile, but the possible significance of the blinding to Aurora is of importance since it prompts her confession of love.

According to Dolores Rosenblum, "Romney Leigh is blinded in order to symbolize the failure of his materialist vision, and to effect his removal from the world of appearances, so that Aurora can never be to him an icon of female beauty or female virtue."[22] For Dorothy Mermin, Romney's blindness signals "the crucial reversal of roles and power between them . . . [Aurora] is no longer the object; she has defined a new space for a woman: as epic protagonist, as speaking subject."[23] And for Susan Friedman, "Romney's blindness represents a symbolic castration of his former patriarchal authority and signals his transformation into a human being capable of love and work in an equitable relationship."[24] Romney's powerlessness paradoxically represents his new strength; it suggests his association with and understanding of the emotional subjective inner world which Barrett Browning has shown to be a source of strength. By being "mulcted as a man" (9.564), Romney assumes those female qualities which—as in the case of Aurora's father—allow him to become whole.

While all these explanations contribute to our understanding of Romney's blindness, they are not entirely satisfactory. Romney's confessions surely make Aurora well aware of these changes in his personality and of the potential for a new, equal relationship between them before she knows him to be blind, and yet she *still* does not declare her love. Even though she recognized that they loved each other, if she had not learned of "this great loss" (9.693), she confesses,

> as I live
> I should have died so, crushing in my hand
> This rose of love, the wasp inside and all,
> Ignoring ever to my soul and you
> Both rose and pain.
>
> (9.689–93)

Possibly it is quite simply the literal fact, as well as the metaphorical implications, of Romney's blindness that needs to be considered. The numerous references to Aurora's tears following the revelation of Romney's blindness appear to link this scene to the other occasion when Aurora weeps after discovering that Marian was raped, not seduced; "weeping in a tender rage" (6.781), Aurora is "convicted, broken utterly" and clings to Marian with "woman's passion" (6.778–79), admitting that she has been wrong. Tears become a visible sign of the release of emotion, of the flooding of passion, of the new ability to respond from the heart. The revelation of Romney's blindness, like Marian's rape, releases emotion and prompts Aurora's tears. It allows her to admit once more that she has been wrong, to respond with "woman's passion," and to say:

> What all this weeping scarce will let me say,
> And yet what women cannot say at all
> But weeping bitterly…(the pride keeps up,
> Until the heart breaks under it)…I love,—
> I love you, Romney.
>
> (9.604–8)

The final celebration of the love between Aurora and Romney reveals some significant differences from the opening celebration of the father's love. Instead of presenting love solely through a male perspective, Barrett Browning attempts to confound or double the perspective. When Aurora concludes her declaration of love she wonders:

> Could I see his face,
> I wept so? Did I drop against his breast,
> Or did his arms constrain me? were my cheeks
> Hot, overflooded, with my tears—or his?
> And which of our two large explosive hearts
> So shook me? That, I know not. There were words
> That broke in utterance…melted, in the fire,—
> Embrace, that was convulsion,…then a kiss
> As long and silent as the ecstatic night,
> And deep, deep, shuddering breaths, which meant beyond
> Whatever could be told by word or kiss.
>
> (9.714–24)

There are two parts to the final description of love. The first, as this passage suggests, is a voiceless communion in which is contained all the emotional, irrational, and spontaneous elements of love suggested by the father's story. But there is no sense of Aurora, as an individual, being overwhelmed or subsumed by love. In a sonnet entitled "Love," Barrett Browning writes that

> When a soul, by choice and conscience, doth
> Throw her full force on another soul,
> The conscience and the concentration both
> Make mere life, Love. For Life in perfect whole
> And aim consummated, is Love in sooth.
>
> (3.179)

This is not a "giving up" of the self, Meredith Raymond points out, but a "casting out"—a small but significant difference.[25] And it is this "casting out" that Aurora enacts when, finally,

> I flung closer to his breast,
> As sword that, after battle, flings to sheath;
> And, in that hurtle of united souls,
> The mystic motions which in common moods
> Are shut beyond our sense, broke in on us,
> And, as we sat, we felt the old earth spin,
> And all the starry turbulence of worlds
> Swing round us in their audient circles, till,
> If that same golden moon were overhead
> Or if beneath our feet, we did not know.
>
> (9.833–42)

Breaking the silent communion in which the outer world has become irrelevant, Romney's voice rises "as some chief musician's song" (9.844) and begins the second part of the description of love. In a form of duet, he and Aurora define their new roles and functions and expand the very boundaries of love itself. No longer seen as the intimate, private enclosure of *Sonnets from the Portuguese,* the "love of wedded souls" (9.882), the counterpart of God's love, becomes a

> Sweet shadow-rose, upon the water of life,
> Of such a mystic substance, Sharon gave
> A name to! human, vital, fructuous rose,
> Whose calyx holds the multitude of leaves,
> Love's filial, loves fraternal, neighbour-loves
> And civic—all fair petals, all good scents,
> All reddened, sweetened from one central Heart.
>
> (9.884–90)

The consummation of their love will lead towards political and social action, to their joint work towards the renewal of the old world and to the building of the new Jerusalem.

This final description of Romney and Aurora "singing" together in a form of duet suggests that their relationship now contains all those elements that Barrett Browning considered most necessary to a successful marriage:

A married life where the partners are *in tune,* is happier than any single life of independent self-love. The difficulty is for the parties to be *in tune*—and to my own private ear, I have not above once or twice or thrice, met with any who were quite so. And oh!—is'nt [sic] it better to live single, than to live miserable, married—with your own solitude in a social state? I think so—I am sure of it. And to look round the world and see how married people live—two in one, instead of one in two! (MRM 2.45).

Aurora Leigh clearly establishes the vital importance of love for Barrett Browning while simultaneously insisting on the importance of a particular type of relationship. Aurora may eventually declare that "Art is much, but Love is more" (9.656), but she must reach a certain stage, a certain position of strength, before she can make such a claim. In tracing her heroine's growth towards an understanding and acceptance of love, and towards a reconciliation of the desires for fulfillment in love and art, Barrett Browning shows how Aurora gradually achieves such a position.

In order to allow women to fulfill themselves both in love and in life, Barrett Browning suggests, it is necessary to replace the socially and culturally established form of male-female relationship, which defines women solely by their roles as wives or mothers, with a new form of relationship which allows women to play a vital active role and which preserves female autonomy. Society's limited views of women's role initially result in Aurora's being forced to choose between love and art; she rejects the traditional confining role of women and chooses instead to fulfill herself through her poetry. Such a choice leads to Aurora's repression of her love for Romney and to a denial of the female side of her personality which causes her to continue to crave his love. Although Barrett Browning clearly shows the futility of Aurora's attempts at denial and repression, repeatedly insists on the incompleteness of life without love, and gradually reveals Aurora's growing unhappiness and the eventual withering of her creativity, the original choice of art over love is nevertheless vindicated. Through her relationships with Marian and Lady Waldemar, Aurora comes to a clearer understanding of the true nature of love, and to an acceptance of her female nature and of female sexuality. Through her writing she proves to Romney her right to pursue her career. Work and experience—rather than mere talk—eventually resolve the dilemma. It is what Aurora learns about love and relationships while she is apart from Romney, and what she communicates to Romney through her art, that ultimately enables them to come together in a relationship where the partners work together "in tune," and live together not as "two in one," but as "one in two."

6

Possession and Control: The *Last Poems*

Aurora Leigh was Elizabeth's last major poetical work. The effort of composition exhausted her; afterward she had almost nothing new to say, and for the remaining four and one-half years of her life she produced only a few short poems, most of which were written to express her sympathy with the Italian cause after the outbreak of fighting in 1859.[1]

While there has been a notable growth of interest in Barrett Browning's work since Gardner Taplin made this rather dismissive pronouncement in his 1957 biography, the absence of much critical commentary on the posthumously published *Last Poems* (1862) suggests continuing agreement that Barrett Browning's poetic career virtually ended with her novel in verse; both Angela Leighton's *Elizabeth Barrett Browning* and Helen Cooper's *Elizabeth Barrett Browning, Woman and Artist* conclude with *Aurora Leigh*. Alethea Hayter, who does briefly discuss *Last Poems*, considers the collection "a puzzle"; it is, she writes, "so various and uneven that it might have been written twenty years apart, or by three or four different poets."[2] In their widely diverse degrees of success as poetry, the eight works which deal specifically with love and sexual relationships in *Last Poems* tend to support Hayter's general observation. There are, however, a number of formal and thematic links among the poems which suggest some measure of consistency in Barrett Browning's final treatment of the subject of love.

Although these eight poems frequently show the influence of Barrett Browning's early experiments with the ballad form, none of them can correctly be identified as a ballad. The type of poem exemplified by such works as "Rhyme of the Duchess May" and "The Romaunt of the Page" has given way to a type of poem which finds its roots in "Bertha in the Lane." The narratorial voice emerges only once, and quickly fades out, and Barrett Browning's interest in elaborate plot lines, in the excitement of a story, has notably diminished. Significantly, the poems are no longer labeled with such tags as "A Romance" or "A Lay"; instead, they generally bear the names of characters. Six are monologues and two are dialogues, and as choice of both title and form would indicate, the emphasis has moved away from narrative—as it did in "Bertha in the Lane"—to the revelation of character and the exploration of emotion; we are not presented with a series of tales, but with a collection of portraits.

In the majority of these poems, as in the earlier monologues delivered by forsaken women, the primary motivation for speech is frustrated desire. This does not, however, confirm Taplin's claim that Barrett Browning had almost nothing new to say. Instead of relying solely on the character of the forsaken woman, she now introduces a group of rather eccentric male speakers, considers a wider range of emotional response, and explores the various effects of the frustration of the lover's desire to possess and control.

Of the eight poems, two are relatively undistinguished works of little depth. "My Kate" and "Amy's Cruelty" are unfortunately marked by what might be called the "Keepsake" manner, and, indeed, they were first published in the *Keepsake* for 1857. "My Kate" in particular displays most of the worst features generally associated with Annual verse; the blandness of the woman described makes it difficult for the reader to muster up much interest in the subject, while the blandness of the style leads one to suspect that Barrett Browning was afflicted by a similar apathy in writing the poem. The faults of "My Kate" are immediately apparent in the opening stanza:

> She was not as pretty as women I know,
> And yet all your best made of sunshine and snow
> Drop to shade, melt to naught in the long trodden ways,
> While she's still remembered on warm and cold days—
> > My Kate.
>
> > (6.20)

The forced and awkward syntax might suggest that Barrett Browning was having trouble finding rhymes, the strained image of "sunshine and snow" is ineffective, and the final line comes dangerously close to doggerel. One searches hopefully, but in vain, for a hint of irony in this lover's eulogy to the woman who spread around sweetness in life—making men nobler, girls purer, and children gladder—with as little apparent effort as she makes the grass grow greener above her grave in death. This final thought, when logically carried through to the notion of the corpse as fertilizer, tends to undermine even the quiet dignity for which the speaker strives.

Although "My Kate" seems of little importance when viewed as an isolated unit, when seen in the larger context of the other poems on love and sexual relationships in *Last Poems*, it contains one point of some interest. Pliant, thoughtful and, above all, good, Kate is no more vocal or active in life than she is in death. The emphasis is on her silence; she exerts influence only through the inner light which shines from her eyes. When she does speak— softly, of course—she says nothing that

> could act
> As a thought or suggestion; she did not attract
> In the sense of the brilliant or wise . . .
> 'Twas her thinking of others made you think of her.

(6.21)

Kate embodies the sentimental ideal of womanhood, and her lover, significantly, is the only speaker in all the eight monologues and dialogues who displays contentment. Every other speaker, with the exception of Amy, who is only fearful, is to some degree dissatisfied, frustrated, or enraged. On the whole, this is a rather angry group of poems. And the constant reiteration of the refrain "My Kate," with its conspicuous possessive, suggests that much of the speaker's satisfaction results from a belief that Kate truly belongs to him. As the sentimental ideal, she makes no disturbing effort to claim independence or autonomy.

Possessiveness, notably, is the cause of Amy's fear in the other *Keepsake* poem, "Amy's Cruelty." In this dialogue, Amy is asked by her neighbor to account for her apparently callous treatment of her lover:

> You give your coffee to the cat,
>   You stroke the dog for coming,
> And all your face grows kinder at
>   The little brown bee's humming.
>
> But when *he* haunts your door...the town
>   Marks coming and marks going...
> You seem to have stiched your eyelids down
>   To that long piece of sewing.

(6.29)

The risks in love, Amy explains, are "terrible and strange." Mouse, bee, dog, and cat are easily satisfied,

> But *he*...to *him*, the least thing given
>   Means great things at a distance;
> He wants my world, my sun, my heaven,
>   Soul, body, whole existence.

(6.30)

The lover's desire to possess his beloved so totally is frightening; Amy is a "simple maiden" unused to such demands, and "this new loving sets the groove / Too much the way of loathing" (6.30). She is quite willing to give herself completely, but first she needs assurance that her lover is willing to give all in return; until then, she must "tremble, doubt,...deny him" (6.30).

Love, Barrett Browning shows in many of these final poems, is inextricably involved with the desire to possess and control. When this desire is thwarted, love can become mixed with, or replaced by, rage, resentment, and bitterness. "May's Love" and "A False Step," while not a great deal more successful as poetry than "My Kate" and "Amy's Cruelty," are nevertheless of more interest for their treatment of frustrated love which turns sour.

The speaker in "A False Step" admits that the woman he loves has stepped on his heart "unaware,— / Malice, not one can impute" (6.5). But the fact that the woman has hurt him unintentionally can neither assuage his pain nor prevent his bitterness. Initially he pretends to be unconcerned and to "disguise" resentment with a transparent air of worldly indifference. The result is a rather nasty sarcasm:

> Sweet, thou hast trod on a heart.
>   Pass; there's a world full of men;
> And women as fair as thou art
>   Must do such things now and then.
>
> Thou only hast stepped unaware,—
>   Malice, not one can impute;
> And why should a heart have been there
>   In the way of a fair woman's foot?
>
>   (6.5)

While the speaker is frustrated in his desire to possess the woman, he nevertheless continues to aspire to some measure of control over her; his love becomes mingled with a vindictive desire to ensure her "false step" will ultimately lead to her unhappiness. With a smug satisfaction, he invites the woman to envision herself old and alone with "the bloom gone away" (6.5):

> Thou'lt sigh, very like, on thy part,
>   "Of all I have known or can know,
> I wish I had only that Heart
>   I trod upon ages ago!"
>
>   (6.6)

Clearly this speech is not simply the private musing of the rejected lover; he is telling the woman what she has done in the hope that someday she will suffer appropriately. The poem belongs to the same tradition as Donne's "The Apparition" ("When by thy scorn, O murderess, I am dead,") and the basic sentiment pervading such poems is "You'll be sorry." Resentment is barely disguised, and the combination of sarcasm and self-pitying smugness eventually moves the reader's sympathy away from the speaker, who would normally be the object of sympathy in such a situation, to the woman who has apparently quite innocently provoked both his love and his malice.

"May's Love" contains a far more vicious attack.[3] The speaker in this poem is incensed by the woman's all-embracing love for everyone and everything, and, although Barrett Browning does not develop the situation to the same extent as Browning, the monologue bears some resemblance to "My Last Duchess." As Browning's Duke is enraged by the wife who "liked whate'er / She looked on, and her looks went everywhere," so Barrett Browning's speaker is maddened by the similarly undiscriminating May: her "world-kissing eyes" lead him to "Loathe the sweet looks dealt to / All things—men and flies" (6.28). The egotism of May's lover pervades the poem; in a manner recalling the final emphatic pronoun in the Duke's reference to the statue "cast in bronze for me," the frustrated lover marks his speech with seven "me"s and two "I"s within fifteen brief lines. Quite unable to tolerate being one among many, he needs to possess May entirely, to capture all her love and all her attention:

> You love all, you say,
>   Round, beneath, above me;
> Find me then some way
>   Better than to love me,
> Me, too, dearest May!
>
> (6.28)

There is a grim sense of barely controlled violence behind his proposed solution:

> You love all, you say,
>   Therefore, Dear, abate me
> Just your love, I pray!
>   Shut your eyes and hate me—
> Only me—fair May!
>
> (6.28)

Formally, both "May's Love" and "A False Step" appear simple, lively, and gay; the feelings which emerge from beneath this deceptively graceful surface, however, are bitter, even brutal. Each poem suggests that thwarted desire has festered within the speaker's mind; love has become distorted, mixed with or even overcome by the rage and bitterness which have been previously contained. The women who do not respond appropriately to the men's desires are subjected to quietly savage attacks. Perhaps it is significant that the more content lover who can speak with ease of "My Kate" (emphasis added) has a beloved who was not only entirely bland and pliant in life, but is also now dead. It is the women with distinct lives of their own, who cannot be possessed and controlled, who provoke the fury of their would-be lovers.

In an article on "Browning and Victorian Poetry of Sexual Love," Isobel Armstrong discusses the appearance of sexual rage in the works of such poets as Patmore, Meredith, Clough, and Tennyson. She traces a pattern in which female docility is repeatedly shown to disguise female duplicity and the recognition of this duplicity leads to male fury. The lover in Patmore's *The Angel in the House,* for example, realizes that woman's apparent submissiveness and innocence is cunningly contrived in order to manipulate man: "To the sweet folly of the dove, / She joins the cunning of the snake" (2.8.i). As Armstrong notes, this "dove-snake manipulating submissiveness" is easily seen through, "and so it is self-defeating, and brings upon the woman only anger and rage."[4]

"Amy's Cruelty" may be seen to provide Barrett Browning's answer to such anger. Female duplicity is here treated with understanding, and Barrett Browning emphasizes that it is forced upon women by conventional male expectations. Amy may be just as manipulative as Patmore's dove-snake, but instead of depicting her as clever and cunning, Barrett Browning shows her tactics to be the inevitable result of fear and the need for self-preservation. When Barrett Browning considers male fury in *Last Poems* it is not shown to be sparked by such duplicity—it results from the failure to possess and control.

Variations on the general theme of the desire to possess and control are explored when Barrett Browning returns more specifically to the question of woman's role in romantic relationships. In two of the most important of the *Last Poems,* "Where's Agnes?" and "Lord Walter's Wife," the men who speak are frustrated primarily by the women's refusal to live up to the demands of the roles in which male fantasy attempts to fix them. The impetus for "Where's Agnes?", one of the more successful poems in the collection, came from Barrett Browning's close friendship and eventual disillusionment with Sophia Eckley, an American who professed to share her deep interest in spiritualism and fabricated various stories about her personal spiritualistic experiences. The relationship between the two women became intimate; Barrett Browning, who admitted to being a "hero and heroine worshipper by religion," with an "organ of veneration . . . as large as a Welsh mountain" (MRM 2.12; 1.145), was quite infatuated with Sophia and completely deceived by her apparently "pure, sweet, and noble nature."[5] (Robert Browning distrusted "speckly Eckley" almost immediately.[6]) When she eventually became aware of Sophia's hypocrisy, Barrett Browning was deeply hurt; writing to Isa Blagden of her "cooled love," she said: "I feel inclined to grind my teeth and stamp. She sticks, dear, like treacle, or dissolved lollipop. Once I praised the sweetness—now I feel very sick at the adhesiveness."[7] In a later letter to Blagden, Robert Browning confirmed that "Where's Agnes?" sprang from his wife's experiences with Sophia, but was "disguised in the circumstances for my sake—who always said 'For the husband's sake,—and because *you* really deserve some punishment in the matter, don't make an explosion.'"[8]

The poem reveals Barrett Browning to be well aware that, as Browning severely states, she got what she deserved "for shutting her eyes and stopping her ears as she determinedly did."[9] But the situation is not only disguised, it is radically transformed. In "Where's Agnes?" Barrett Browning adapts her experiences to take a satiric look at a young man disillusioned by the woman he considered no less than an angel from heaven. The poem is in many ways reminiscent of Swift's boudoir poems which satirize such idealistic swains as Cassinus and Strephon when they are horrified to discover concrete evidence of their nymphs' undeniable earthiness. It is not a poem of moral outrage which reproves a fickle and deceptive woman, but an exposé of the infatuated and naive lover.

The speaker readily admits that he originally had some doubts concerning Agnes. "What good, I thought, is done / By such sweet things, if any" (6.36). Her only "virtues" are her soft low voice, melting curves, and angelic face; she makes no claim to any deeper moral virtues. But asking himself "What if God has set her here / Less for action than for Being?— / For the eye and for the ear" (6.37), the lover dismisses his fears. On the basis of her physical beauty alone, he invests Agnes, his "white rose" (6.38), with a moral significance that she simply does not possess; he applies to her the clichéd romantic notion that woman's divine mission is to lead man to God:

> Just to show what beauty may
>> Just to prove what music can,—
> And then to die away
>> From the presence of a man,
> Who shall learn, henceforth, to pray.
>
> As a door, left half ajar
>> In heaven, would make him think
> How heavenly different are
>> Things glanced at through the chink,
> Till he pined from near to far.
>
>   (6.37)

This romantic idea with its Platonic origins is never supported by Barrett Browning; it is no more than a variation on the previously dismissed cloud-minding theory which so firmly relegates women to the status of objects. Love is not seen by Barrett Browning as a kind of metaphorical ladder leading the lover to heaven; she is more concerned with a love that shows, to adapt the image she used to describe Browning's poetry, "a heart within blood-tinctured, of a veined humanity" (2.292).

As the speaker's descriptions of Agnes demonstrate, there is more than a touch of irony in Barrett Browning's presentation of the idealistic lover who constructs a faultless angel out of a pair of clear gray eyes and some fluffy wisps of hair:

> She wore her hair away
>   From her forehead,—like a cloud
> Which a little wind in May
>   Peels off finely: disallowed
> Though bright enough to stay.
>
> For the heavens must have the place
>   To themselves, to use and shine in,
> As her soul would have her face
>   To press through upon mine, in
> That orb of angel grace.

(6.35)

The forced style, awkward syntax, and hazy religious language clearly undermine the over-enthusiastic fantasies of the enthralled lover who strains after a sufficiently elevated image with which to capture the essence of his beloved. And the excessive use of exclamatory emphasis takes the speaker's laments into the realm of parody:

> My Agnes,—mine!
> Called so! felt of too much worth
>   To be used so! too divine
> To be breathed near, and so forth!

(6.37)

That humorous concluding "and so forth" sweepingly embraces all the remaining clichés.

The speaker's initial reaction to the news that his Agnes now deserves to be named with *"that word"* is disbelief (6.38). His first word is a decisive "Nay" (6.34); the very thought is absurd:

> My Agnes false? such shame?
>   She? Rather be it said
> That the pure saint of her name
>   Has stood there in her stead,
> And tricked you to this blame.

(6.34)

His defense of the woman, however, can rest only on the superficial evidence provided by her physical appearance—the clearness of her eyes, the chaste draping of her clothes, the angelic orb of her face. The woman he so insistently and possessively calls "My Agnes,—mine!" is indeed false—she has never existed.

But the speaker's final acceptance of the "falseness" of Agnes is not a recognition that the woman he has created is only an imaginary construct. He is instead angered by her failure to live up to the role in which he has attempted to fix her; the woman he believed to be sent like an angel falls like the woman she actually is. His disillusionment leads him, in the manner of Swift's young men, to swerve violently from one extreme to the other: Agnes is now seen not as saint or angel, but as a she-devil who can lead man only to hell. The woman who "scarcely trod the earth" is "Turned mere dirt" (6.37).

Disillusionment with Agnes results in a more wide-spread unhappiness with beauty in general; the speaker rejects all superficial attraction as deceptive: "Then the great joys of the Lord / Do not last?" he concludes in dismay, "Then all this paint / Runs off nature? leaves a board?" (6.30). With an angry and emphatic rejection of all feminine beauty, the disappointed lover concludes:

> Then henceforth may earth grow trees!
> No more roses!—hard straight lines
> To score lies out! none of these
> Fluctuant curves, but firs and pines,
> Poplars, cedars, cypresses.
>
> (6.39)

Barrett Browning's male characters in these final lyrics frequently appear to be straw men embodying particular principles that she sets up for the express purpose of knocking down. The fatuous lover represents a particular type taken to extremes in order to reveal the ridiculous nature of any such attempt to fix women in pre-determined and clichéd roles.

This is also true in "Lord Walter's Wife," a dialogue which provides an appropriate counterpart to "Where's Agnes?" The poem records an exchange between two characters known only by their functions as Maude's fiancé and Lord Walter's wife. The young man has been indulging in an elaborate game of flirtation with his friend's wife, expecting from her no more than passive acceptance of her role as object in his sexual fantasies. Finding his insinuations insulting, the wife determines to teach him a lesson by appearing to agree to an affair. While the infatuated lover of Agnes creates an illusory pure angel, this lover has transformed Lord Walter's wife into the other side of the cliché— the dangerous temptress. In each case, the woman as an individual is basically ignored; it is a fantasy figure with which the man is concerned; both women explode these imaginary constructs, the first through sexual betrayal, the second by forcing an apparent reconciliation between the illusory and the real.

In 1861, Barrett Browning sent the poem to Thackeray for the *Cornhill;* after some delay, Thackeray uneasily returned the poem with the following explanation:

You see that our Magazine is written not only for men and women but for boys, girls, infants, sucklings almost; and one of the best wives, mothers, women in the world writes some verses which I feel certain would be objected to by many of our readers. Not that the writer is not pure, and the moral most pure, chaste, and right, but there are things my squeamish public will not hear on Monday, though on Sundays they listen to them without scruple. In your poem, you know, there is an account of unlawful passion, felt by a man for a woman, and though you write pure doctrine, and real modesty, and pure ethics, I am sure our readers would make an outcry, and so I have not published this poem. (EBB 2.444)

There is an undeniable hint of delight in Barrett Browning's reaction to this letter. "Thackeray has turned me out of the *Cornhill* for indecency" she told Sarianna Browning (EBB 2.443). To Thackeray himself she replied in a similar vein: "Never was anyone turned out of the room for indecent behaviour in a more gracious and conciliatory manner" (EBB 2.445). But Barrett Browning's defense of her poem focuses not so much on the idea of simple "unlawful passion," but on the more general question of the treatment of women which is implied by the poem:

I am not a "fast woman." I don't like coarse subjects, or the coarse treatment of any subject. But I am deeply convinced that the corruption of our society requires not shut doors and windows, but light and air: and that it is exactly because pure and prosperous women choose to *ignore* vice, that miserable women suffer wrong by it everywhere. Has paterfamilias, with his Oriental traditions and veiled female faces, very successfully dealt with a certain class of evil? What if materfamilias, with her quick sure instincts and honest innocent eyes, do more towards their expulsion by simply looking at them and calling them by their names? (EBB 2.445)

Barrett Browning's reference to this "certain class of evil" is rather ambiguous. The "vice" which by being ignored leads "miserable women" to suffer wrong is clearly not just adultery—the unlawful passion to which Thackeray objects. Both letter and poem are more concerned with the general subject of the "use" of women as vehicles for male sexual fantasies and with the tendency to divide women into the clichéd roles of pure woman and dangerous temptress.

The poem begins with a pertinent comment from the narrator: "'But why do you go?' said the lady, while both sat under the yew, / And her eyes were alive in their depth, as the kraken beneath the sea-blue" (6.9). There is certainly the suggestion of hidden, lurking danger in this description of the lady's eyes, but it is not the illusory type of danger typically associated with the femme fatale—it is a very real warning; Lord Walter's wife is about to put the young man firmly in his place, to prove to him that "whate'er you might dream or avow / By illusion, you wanted precisely no more of me than you have now" (6.13).

The young man's initial response to the lady's invitation is marked by the "frivolous cant" (6.13) which has previously characterized his flirtations with this "siren." He must go "'Because I fear you,' he answered;—'because you are far too fair, / And able to strangle my soul in a mesh of your gold-coloured hair'" (6.9). Lord Walter's wife, impatient with such nonsense, quickly brings the exchange down to earth: "'Oh, that,' she said, 'is no reason! Such knots are quickly undone, / And too much beauty, I reckon, is nothing but too much sun'" (6.9). As her invitations become more direct, the young man becomes more alarmed. He reminds her of Lord Walter, of Maude, and finally of her daughter: "'But you,' he replied, 'have a daughter, a young little child, who was laid / In your lap to be pure; so I leave you: the angels would make me afraid'" (6.10). His increasingly inventive excuses have pointed out exactly what the woman wants him to consider—that she is Lord Walter's wife and he is Maude's fiancé. She brings his implied desires into the open, but forces him to reconcile these desires with an acceptance of their actual positions. Eventually, he is goaded into anger: "Why, now, you no longer are fair! / Why, now, you no longer are fatal, but ugly and hateful, I swear" (6.11). It is quite fitting that the young man has begun to sound less like an ardent lover than a petulant little boy, frustrated in his desire to play a favorite game; his attitude towards women is both insulting and immature. While he has not the slightest intention of actually entering into an affair with his friend's wife, he has derived a great deal of furtive pleasure from imagining such an affair; Lord Walter's wife, as she informs him with the utmost contempt, has been well aware of his thoughts: "You bring us your vices so near / That we smell them! You think in our presence a thought 'twould defame us to hear!" (6.11):

> You grew, sir, pale to impertinence, once when I showed you a ring
> You kissed my fan when I dropped it. No matter!—I've broken the thing.
>
> You did me the honour, perhaps, to be moved at my side now and then
> In the senses—a vice, I have heard, which is common to beasts and some men.
>
> (6.12–13)

While the young man views Maude as the pure and virtuous woman he plans to marry, he considers Lord Walter's wife as the dangerously beautiful woman who tempts him to give in to what, as the above passage clearly reveals, is no more than lust. By placing her in such a role, he implies that Lord Walter's wife would be willing to indulge in an affair and that he must try to resist her wiles. Naturally, she objects to such insinuations: "You take us for harlots, I tell you, and not for the women we are" (6.14). His behavior, she claims, makes a mockery of the pure love which is "a virtue for heroes!—as white as the snow on high hills" (6.13), and, insisting that he look at her "full in the face! in the face" (6.14), she calls for honesty and straightforwardness in relationships between men and women.

While Lord Walter's wife displays both anger and scorn in her refusal to be used as the object of the young man's sexual fantasies, the question of female rage and bitterness is more closely examined when Barrett Browning returns to the question of woman's voice and to the lament of the forsaken woman. There are two attempts to deal with this subject in *Last Poems:* "Void in Law," and "Bianca among the Nightingales," one of the finest short love lyrics Barrett Browning ever wrote.

One of the obstacles to the clear and direct expression of desire in Barrett Browning's early experiments with the lament is the need to account for the various contradictory emotions which are necessarily present when desire is voiced subsequent to union and separation. The woman's persistent love would lead her to desire continuing possession of the beloved, Barrett Browning suggests, and the frustration of this desire would result in bitterness and resentment. In the traditional male lyric—which voices desire as it is experienced prior to any consummation—this is not usually a consideration; such works as Suckling's "Song," with its impatient and dismissive "The devil take her!" are clearly reversing Petrarchan conventions. In the lament of the forsaken woman, however, inevitable bitterness and resentment need to be considered. Simply ignoring such emotions tends to lead to the production of such sentimental verses as Mulock's "Only a Woman": the woman becomes love's martyr, and man's infidelity simply serves to reveal the glorious nature of woman's love. Barrett Browning resolves the dilemma in "A Romance of the Ganges" by allowing love to be overwhelmed by rage, and in "Change upon Change," "That Day," and "Bertha in the Lane" by presenting love side by side with bitterness. Now, in "Void in Law" and "Bianca among the Nightingales," she attempts two quite different approaches.

"Void in Law" has as much in common with such poems as "May's Love" and "A False Step" as with the early experiments with the forsaken woman; Barrett Browning's concern is to show how the bitterness and rage resulting from the thwarted desire to possess can fester and eventually distort love. The wife in this poem has been deserted by her husband upon the discovery of a technical flaw in the wedding ceremony; the marriage has been annulled, and the husband has taken advantage of his legal right to leave wife and child and has married another woman, a woman who, since "the world take her part, / Saying 'She was the woman to choose'" (6.7), is in some way more socially acceptable.

The wife's monologue takes the form of a lullaby that she sings to her child; as it begins, she is attempting to induce the child to sleep:

> Sleep, little babe, on my knee,
>   Sleep, for the midnight is chill,
> And the moon has died out in the tree,
>   And the great human world goeth ill.
> Sleep, for the wicked agree:

> Sleep, let them do as they will.
>   Sleep.
>
> (6.6)

Although this opening stanza reveals the wife's unhappiness, it is still soft and soothing. With the regular rhythm, the systematic pauses, and the anaphoric use of "Sleep," the lines aptly reflect the smooth and gentle rocking motion of the woman cradling her child as she sings. Her own troubles, however, are not forgotten:

> Sleep, thou has drawn from my breast
>   The last drop of milk that was good;
> And now, in a dream, suck the rest,
>   Lest the real should trouble thy blood.
> Suck, little lips dispossessed,
>   As we kiss in the air whom we would.
>   Sleep.
>
> (6.6)

The child is her only consolation, but as "the divine / Seal of right upon loves that deserve" (6.7), it is also a constant reminder of the wrongs that she has suffered. As the child's lips, so like the father's, remind her that her lips too are "dispossessed," the woman's increasing distress is reflected in her lullaby. Rage and resentment have combined with love to produce a metaphorical bitter milk, and the poem, the lullaby, becomes the receptacle into which this bitter milk is released.

The smooth flowing lines of the opening stanza give way to agitation and short, jerking clauses, and the deserted woman reveals her determination to "Cling on to him, never to loose" (6.7):

> He thinks that, when done with this place,
>   All's ended? he'll new-stamp the ore?
> Yes, Caesar's—but not in our case.
>   Let him learn we are waiting before
> The grave's mouth, the heaven's gate, God's face,
>   With implacable love evermore.
>   Sleep.
>
> (6.8)

The woman's love has mixed with her jealousy, rage, and bitterness to produce a monstrous, grim possessiveness:

> He's ours, though he kissed her but now,
>   He's ours, though she kissed in reply;
> He's ours, though himself disavow,
>   And God's universe favour the lie;
> Ours to claim, ours to clasp, ours below,
>   Ours above,...if we live, if we die.
>   Sleep.

(6.8)

The regularity and repetition of these lines suggests a correspondence with the opening stanza, but the lullaby now appears less a soothing song directed at the child than a fierce placation of her own needs; she is determined to cling on to her divine right to claim the errant husband as "ours." Ironically, the release of pent-up emotion results in rage and bitterness being vented upon the child, and, recognizing this, the woman attempts to smooth over her "rough song" (6.8); "If the one who remains (only one) / Set her grief at thee, turned in a heat / To thine enemy,—were it well done?" (6.8–9).

In "Void in Law," the conflicting emotions of the deserted wife combine to produce a bitter milk, an "implacable love," and the voice of desire is characterized by a fierce and relentless possessiveness. Considering the situation described, the poem could easily have degenerated into sentimentality; there is, however, no touch of the sentimental; the deserted wife is not even presented in a totally sympathetic light. As a woman abandoned in favor of a more socially acceptable wife, and in her venting of her anger upon the child, the wife in "Void in Law" provides a reminder that another prototype of the forsaken woman, although not as influential as Dido and Ariadne, is Euripides's Medea.

Instead of combining the various conflicting emotions in "Bianca among the Nightingales," Barrett Browning divides and isolates them; the inevitable bitterness and resentment of the abandoned woman is channelled away from the fickle lover and directed solely at the other woman; as a result, the female lyric voice of desire emerges purely and clearly. Bianca has been deserted by her fiancé, Giulio, who has left Italy to be with an Englishwoman. Although she has ample reason to direct her rage at her fickle lover, Bianca never even suggests that she has been forsaken; she chooses instead to claim that "we two / Are sundered" (6.16)—with the implications of "sundered" being wrenched or torn apart. And the only time she uses the word "false," it is applied not to Giulio, but to the Englishwoman who is, Bianca claims, "A worthless woman; mere cold clay / As all false things are" (6.18).

Considering her situation, it is doubtful whether an interpretation of the poem can be based upon her assessment of the Englishwoman's character. There is no possibility of testing the accuracy of her accusations, but it is clear that Giulio made a conscious choice; no man is "beguiled" against his will in the manner suggested by Bianca.[10] "The woman is so fair, / She takes the breath of men away / Who gaze upon her unaware" (6.18), Bianca claims, transforming the woman into a kind of Medusa figure, and consequently relieving Giulio of all responsibility for his actions.[11]

Like most of Barrett Browning's heroines, Bianca is convinced that love is forever; the love which remains alive within her memory is unchangeable, and she continues to believe what Giulio vowed: "God's Ever guaranties this Now" (6.15):

> I think I hear him, how he cried
>   "My own soul's life!" between their notes.
> Each man has but one soul supplied,
>   And that's immortal. Though his throat's
> On fire with passion now, to *her*
>   He can't say what to me he said!
>
>   (6.16)

Giulio may feel physical passion for the other woman, but Bianca is convinced that their relationship does not constitute love; Giulio's love will always belong to her. If, as she has been told, he moves the other woman, it must necessarily be on a superficial level:

> He says to her what moves her most.
>   He would not name his soul within
> Her hearing,—rather pays her cost
>   With praises to her lips and chin.
> Man has but one soul, 'tis ordained,
>   And each soul but one love, I add.
>
>   (6.16)

But while Bianca can confidently assert that Giulio's love for her must remain constant, she is still faced with the undeniable fact that she is alone, that "souls are damned and love's profaned" (6.16).

It is Bianca's refusal to accept the possibility that love could change or end which leads her to place all the blame on the other woman. As long as Giulio is seen to be captivated against his will, she can continue to believe in the existence of his love, and as long as she can redirect her rage and bitterness away from Giulio, she can maintain the purity and intensity of her own love for him.

The sensuous nature of their love is vividly captured in the three opening stanzas of "Bianca among the Nightingales." There is little left of the deserted maiden in Barrett Browning's presentation of Bianca; she is a woman abandoned not only *by* Giulio, but also *to* her emotions. The trappings of self-restraint and self-denial have quite disappeared, love is directly and violently expressed, and the speaker is clearly no maiden, but a sexually experienced woman capable of giving voice to mature and passionate desire:

> The cypress stood up like a church
>   That night we felt our love would hold,
> And saintly moonlight seemed to search
>   And wash the whole world clean as gold;
> The olives crystallized the vales'
>   Broad slopes until the hills grew strong:
> The fire-flies and the nightingales
>   Throbbed each to either, flame and song.
> The nightingales, the nightingales!
>
> (6.14–15)

In the opening reference to the cypress, sexual and religious imagery merge to produce a vibrant sense of strength and vitality; the symbolic value of the tree, however, simultaneously provides an ominous reminder of death and sorrow. Everything in this sensuous landscape, trees, insects, and birds, reflects the physical desire of the lovers, and as the moonlight brightens the night, it sanctifies the relationship, merging the physical with the spiritual. This mingling of the physical and the spiritual continues in the following stanza as the cypress is described standing upon "the angle of its shade . . . / Half up, half down, as double made, / Along the ground, against the sky" (6.15). The lovers too experience "Such leaps of blood, so blindly driven, / We scarce knew if our nature meant / Most passionate earth or intense heaven" (6.15).

Bianca is reliving the fierce passion that she experienced at the moment of sexual consummation. While this consummation cannot be directly described by Barrett Browning, it is nevertheless quite clearly suggested, particularly in the following image of piercing arrows:

> We paled with love, we shook with love,
>   We kissed so close we could not vow;
> Till Giulio whispered "Sweet, above
>   God's Ever guaranties this Now."
> And through his words the nightingales
>   Drove straight and full their long clear call,
> Like arrows through heroic mails,
>   And love was awful in it all.
> The nightingales, the nightingales!
>
> (6.15)

The strikingly intense rendition of passion in the opening of "Bianca among the Nightingales" is aptly captured in that summarizing phrase—"And love was awful in it all." It is this love, and more specifically, Giulio's vow of eternal love, that is associated in Bianca's mind with the song of the nightingales; the piercing call and Giulio's words become inextricably bound together. For the reader who associates the nightingale with Philomela, and man's treachery in love, the song may be a sinister portent of Bianca's fate. The image of the cry piercing Giulio's words like "arrows through heroic mails" assumes destructive as well as sensuous connotations.

In "Bianca among the Nightingales," as in the previous poems concerning forsaken women, frustrated love imposes distance, and distance intensifies desire. Bianca has attempted to overcome the actual distance placed between her and Giulio by his desertion. She "yearned after" him in her "desperate need / And followed him as he did her / To coasts left bitter by the tide" (6.15). But standing in the Englishwoman's garden chamber, she is no closer to Giulio than she was in Italy:

> O cold white moonlight of the north,
>   Refresh these pulses, quench this hell!
> O coverture of death drawn forth
>   Across this garden-chamber...well!
> But what have nightingales to do
>   In gloomy England, called the free...
> (Yes, free to die in!...) when we two
>   Are sundered, singing still to me?
> And still they sing, the nightingales!
>
> (6.15–16)

The passion that Bianca experiences reveals itself in both her physical torments and her mental aberrations. Her pulse races wildly, her body is suffused with torturous heat, she is emotionally overwrought, swinging wildly between passionate expressions of love and vindictive expressions of hate, and her judgment is clearly impaired—she is quite unable to recognize the obvious shortcomings of her "only good" (6.19), her beloved Giulio.

The metaphorical distance between Bianca and Giulio, unlike the actual distance, can potentially be overcome. As long as Bianca holds on to the memory of love and her conviction of its continuing existence, she can maintain both her ties with Giulio and her sanity. Her confidence in this love, however, is suddenly undermined when she hears the nightingales sing in the English garden. She cannot understand why they should sing now that she and Giulio are "sundered," or why they should appear as happy here among the fogs and "dull round blots of foliage" (6.17) as they were among the Tuscan trees. The implications of their appearance are disturbing; Bianca must consider that Giulio too is "content . . . in this land" (6.17). As far as the nightingales' song continues to represent love, it now seems possible that it represents the new love of Giulio and the Englishwoman—a love Bianca needs to believe does not exist. For Bianca, therefore, the song begins to assume its conventional associations with man's treachery.

Barrett Browning makes highly effective use of the refrain in "Bianca among the Nightingales." In such early works as "Rhyme of the Duchess May," the ballad refrain is only barely functional, and, by the time "Toll slowly" has been repeated one hundred and twelve times, it has become painfully monotonous. Here, the refrain is an integral part of the poem, and Barrett Browning exploits the very tendency of refrains to grow intolerable, to infuriate and madden the listener.

Although Bianca determines to ignore the song that acts as a refrain for her—"I will not hear these nightingales" (6.17)—it continues to reverberate in her head and to undermine her confidence in love. The actual refrain of the poem, rather than the fixed song to which it refers, is aptly varied to reflect Bianca's growing frustration. From its simple beginning as "The nightingales, the nightingales!" it shifts to the more distraught cry of "And still they sing, the nightingales," and to the desperate plea of "Our Lady hush these nightingales" (6.19).

As Bianca's frustration increases, her attacks upon the other woman grow more vicious. She dehumanizes her rival, transforming her into a predator and Giulio into her prey. With her sweet voice and "fine tongue" she hunted Giulio, Bianca claims, as "snakes indeed / Kill flies" or "Like spiders, in the altar's wood." The Englishwoman is guilty of "sacrilege"; she "lied and stole, / And spat into my love's pure pyx / The rank saliva of her soul" (6.18–19). Bianca reveals her own venom in these attacks; the intensity of her hatred for the woman at least matches, if it does not exceed, the intensity of her continuing love for Giulio.

As she recognizes that her preoccupation with the woman causes her to "join her . . . with Giulio, in each word I say," Bianca decides to "Let her pass" (6.19), and achieves some measure of calm; the final stanza begins with a poignant sense of quiet agony as she calls for the last time upon her lover:

> Giulio, my Giulio!—sing they so,
>   And you be silent? Do I speak,
> And you not hear? An arm you throw
>   Round some one, and I feel so weak?

(6.19)

Giulio's silence and his deafness to her pleas appear to have led Bianca to an acceptance of her absolute separation from her lover; his new love leaves her weak and alone. The nightingales' song has insidiously undermined her confidence in the love to which she has desperately clung. In one last passionate outburst, Bianca vents her rage upon the birds which, as they continue to "torture and deride" (6.18), are now associated with the ill-omened owl, the representative not of love, but of death and despair:

> —Oh, owl-like birds! They sing for spite,
>   They sing for hate, they sing for doom,
> They'll sing through death who sing through night,
>   They'll sing and stun me in the tomb—
> The nightingales, the nightingales!
>
> (6.20)

The violent and angry sense of frustration which marks this concluding stanza emerges as the dominant tone in the majority of Barrett Browning's *Last Poems* on the subject of love and sexual relationships. A desire to possess and control is shown to be a fundamental element in the love experienced by the speakers, and the thwarting of this desire repeatedly results in bitterness, rage, and resentment. Barrett Browning's primary concerns with woman's role in love relationships and woman's voice in love poetry are linked in *Last Poems* by this common theme of the lover's need to possess and control the beloved. The male speakers are frustrated when women refuse to accept the roles in which male fantasy attempts to fix them. The two betrayed women cling determinedly to the illusion of continuing love, of continuing possession, and provide two variations on the female lyric voice of desire: one is monstrously grim, and the other passionately abandoned, a woman torn apart by the memories of sexual consummation and the reality of sexual frustration.

Notes

Chapter 1

1. Virginia Woolf, *The Common Reader, Second Series* (London: Hogarth, 1932), 202.

2. Woolf, 202.

3. Ellen Moers, *Literary Women* (New York: Doubleday, 1976), 40.

4. The most notable exceptions to this prevailing trend are Angela Leighton's discussion of the sonnets and some ballads in her recent *Elizabeth Barrett Browning* (Bloomington: Indiana University Press, 1986) and Dorothy Mermin's two articles—"Barrett Browning's Stories," *Browning Institute Studies* 13 (1985), 99–112; "The Female Poet and the Embarrassed Reader: Elizabeth Barrett Browning's *Sonnets from the Portuguese,*" *ELH* 48.2 (1981): 351–67. Helen Cooper's recent *Elizabeth Barrett Browning, Woman and Artist* (Chapel Hill: University of North Carolina Press, 1988) has very little to say about the sonnets.

5. *The Letters of Elizabeth Barrett Browning,* ed. Frederic G. Kenyon, 2 vols. (London: Smith, 1891) 1.230–32. Hereafter cited in text as EBB.

6. Margaret Homans, "'Syllables of Velvet': Dickinson, Rossetti, and the Rhetorics of Sexuality," *Feminist Studies* 11.3 (1985): 574.

7. Felicia Hemans, *The Poetical Works* (London: Warne n.d.), 263. All further references to this edition will be cited in text by page number.

8. Dolores Rosenblum, *Christina Rossetti: The Poetry of Endurance* (Carbondale: Southern Illinois University Press, 1986), 9.

9. *The Letters of Elizabeth Barrett Browning to Mary Russell Mitford: 1836–54,* ed. Meredith B. Raymond and Mary Rose Sullivan, 3 vols. (Waco, Tex.: Armstrong Browning Library, 1983) 2.260. Hereafter cited in text as MRM.

10. Letitia Elizabeth Landon, *Poetical Works,* 2 vols. (London: Longman, 1853) 1.47. All further references to this edition will be cited by volume and page number in the text.

11. For further discussion of this point see Rosenblum, 10–14.

12. Letitia Elizabeth Landon, *The Venetian Bracelet and Other Poems* (London: Longman, 1829), vi.

13. *Venetian Bracelet*, vi.

14. Rosenblum, 12.

Chapter 2

1. *Letters Addressed to Richard Hengist Horne*, ed. S. Mayer (New York: Knox, 1877), 52. Although Barrett Browning does not seem to have experienced any major romantic disappointments herself, she does appear to have been at least mildly infatuated with the Greek scholar H. S. Boyd during the early thirties, and her affections were clearly not returned as she wished. Comparing herself to a hot iron on which Boyd repeatedly threw cold water, she wrote in her diary, "I wish that water *would* make my iron as cold as itself." *Diary by E. B. B.: The Unpublished Diary of Elizabeth Barrett Barrett, 1831–1832*, ed. Philip Kelley and Ronald Hudson (Athens, Ohio: Ohio University Press, 1969), 37.

2. *The Letters of Robert Browning and Elizabeth Barrett Barrett 1845–1846*, ed. Elvan Kintner, 2 vols. (Cambridge, Mass.: Harvard University Press, 1969) 1.48. Hereafter cited in text as RB.

3. *The Complete Works of Elizabeth Barrett Browning*, ed. Charlotte Porter and Helen A. Clarke, 6 vols. (New York: Crowell, 1900; AMS Reprint 1973) 1.161. Barrett Browning's poetry is hereafter cited in the text by volume and page number.

4. Dorothy Mermin, "Elizabeth Barrett Browning through 1844: Becoming a Woman Poet," *Studies in English Literature* 26.4 (1986): 730.

5. Mermin, "Elizabeth Barrett Browning through 1844," 730.

6. "A Man's Requirements," "A Woman's Shortcomings" and "Change upon Change" were all first published in *Blackwood's* in 1846. They belong, however, to the period prior to *Sonnets from the Portuguese*, and I will consider them in this context. Barrett Browning told Mitford that just prior to eloping with Browning, she sent in these verses which belonged "to old feelings and impressions" (MRM 3.195).

7. Angela Leighton has provided an illuminating discussion of the poem in her *Elizabeth Barrett Browning* (Bloomington: Indiana University Press, 1986), 34–37.

8. Like many of her ballads, "The Lay of the Brown Rosary" was written to accompany a specific illustration; this time, however, Barrett Browning took so many liberties with the situation she was given to work with that the artist had to alter all the frame figures in order to accommodate Barrett Browning's fanciful additions. (MRM 2.382).

9. [Mitford, Mary Russell], *Findens' Tableaux of National Character, Beauty, and Costume*, rpt. 2 vols. (London: March, 1843), 2.155–59.

10. Onora's relationship with the nun, representative of sexual love, and St. Agnes, representative of spiritual love, anticipates Aurora's relationship with Lady Waldemar and Marian in *Aurora Leigh*. The poem vaguely suggests that nun and saint may be aspects of Onora's own character.

11. The reference to a three-year-old dead child is reminiscent of Onora's wish to lie beneath the linden tree; both represent unrealistic desire for naive innocence rather than mature experience.

12. See Dorothy Mermin's discussion of these early poems in "Barrett Browning's Stories," *Browning Institute Studies* 13 (1985): 99–112.

13. To avoid confusion between her ellipses and mine, I single space those belonging to Barrett Browning.

14. Unfortunately, in her eagerness to demonstrate her point, Barrett Browning begins her argument in this fragment on shaky ground. At sixteen, she had already read enough to know that women had frequently been chosen as subjects by the poets—and not just in the domestic sphere she scorns; her point cries out for some qualification—as it is, it tends to undermine the valid point she goes on to make concerning woman's role.

15. "Fragment of an 'Essay on Woman,'" *Studies in Browning and His Circle* 12 (1984): 11–12.

16. John Ruskin, "Of Queens' Gardens," *Sesame and Lilies* (London: Dent, 1911), 59.

17. Phillip David Sharp, *Poetry in Progress: Elizabeth Barrett Browning and the Sonnets Notebook*, diss. Louisiana State University, 1977, 98.

18. Lord Viscount Strangford, *Poems, from the Portuguese of Luis de Camoens* (London: Carpenter, 1805), 7–11. Strangford's translation of Camoens' Spanish "Mi coracon me han roubado"—"The heart that warmed my guileless breast," contains the refrain used in Barrett Browning's "Catarina to Camoens": "And sweetest eyes that e'er were seen!" It does not appear in Camoens' original. See Monica Letzring, "Strangford's *Poems from the Portuguese of Luis de Camoens*," *Comparative Literature* 23.4 (1971): 304–5.

19. See the 1838 draft of "Catarina to Camoens" in *The Poet's Enchiridion*, ed. H. Buxton Forman (Boston: Bibliophile, 1914), 47–49. Both texts use seven stanzas of seven lines; both use the rhyme scheme *ababcc*; and while there are some variations in meter, both use iambs in alternate lines of tetrameter and trimeter.

20. Marianne Shapiro, "The Provençal Trobairitz and the Limits of Courtly Love," *Signs* 3.3 (1978): 562.

21. Edgar Allan Poe, "The Philosophy of Composition," *The Complete Poems and Stories of Edgar Allan Poe, with Selections from His Critical Writings*, ed. A. H. Quinn (New York: Knopf, 1951), 982.

22. Dinah Mulock, *Thirty Years: Being Poems, New and Old* (Boston: Houghton, n.d.), 228.

23. Mulock, 231.

24. S. J. Hale, ed. *The Ladies Wreath* (Boston: Marsh, 1837), 147.

25. Letitia Landon, *Poetical Works*, 2 vols. (London: Longman, 1853), 1.272.

26. Mary Russell Mitford, *The Life of Mary Russell Mitford: Told by Herself in Letters to Her Friends*, ed. Rev. A. G. K. L'Estrange, 2 vols. (New York: Harper, 1870), 2.197.

27. [Mitford], *Findens' Tableaux*, 1.37–38.

28. Mermin, "Barrett Browning's Stories", 102.

29. A version of this discussion of "Bertha in the Lane" has been published in *Browning Society Notes* 16.3 (1986/87): 3–9.

30. Roger Lancelyn Green, ed. *A Book of British Ballads* (London: Dent, 1966), 6.

31. Letitia Landon, "The Secret Discovered," *Friendship's Offering* (1837), 320–34.

32. Review of *Poems* (1844), *Blackwood's Magazine* 56 (1844): 626.

33. [Chorley] Review of *Poems* (1844), *Athenaeum* (1844): 1244.

34. Review of *Poems* (1844), *Westminster Review* 42 (1844): 387.

35. Sandra Gilbert and Susan Gubar, *The Madwoman in the Attic* (New Haven: Yale University Press, 1979), 463. Dorothy Mermin, although she does not develop the point, has noted that the poem is a dramatic monologue; see "Barrett Browning's Stories," 105.

36. See Leighton, 63–65 for a discussion of the mother-daughter relationship in this poem.

37. Compare Shakespeare's similar use of rosemary as a bridal flower thrown on the corpses of Ophelia and Juliet.

38. Gilbert and Gubar, 25.

Chapter 3

1. A version of this chapter has previously appeared in *Victorian Poetry* (March 1989).

2. See for example, Alethea Hayter, *Mrs. Browning: A Poet's Work and its Setting* (London: Faber, 1962), 85–86; Virginia Radley, *Elizabeth Barrett Browning* (New York: Twayne, 1972), 60–62.

3. The notable exception is "Bertha in the Lane," which, like Lady Geraldine's Courtship," is a monologue.

4. Poe, for example, claimed: "With the exception of Tennyson's 'Locksley Hall,' we have never pursued a poem combining so much of the fiercest passion with so much of the most ethereal fancy, as the 'Lady Geraldine's Courtship' of Miss Barrett. We are forced to admit, however, that the latter work *is* a very palpable imitation of the former, which it surpasses in plot or rather in thesis, as much as it falls below it in artistical management, and a certain calm energy." Review of *Poems* (1844), *Broadway Journal* (1845): 17.

5. Edmund Stedman, *Victorian Poets* (Boston: Houghton, 1891), 130–31.

6. [Patmore] Review of *Aurora Leigh* and other poems, *North British Review* 26 (1857): 445.

7. This is, of course, what Patmore himself produces in *The Angel in the House*.

8. [Patmore], 445.

Chapter 4

1. Edmund Stedman, *Victorian Poets* (Boston: Houghton, 1891), 138.

2. Review of *Last Poems*, *Dublin University Magazine* 60 (1862): 162.

3. Stedman, 137; Kate Field, "Elizabeth Barrett Browning," *Atlantic Monthly* 8.47 (1861): 369; William Caldwell Roscoe, *Poems and Essays*, ed. Richard Hutton, 2 vols. (London: Chapman Hall, 1860), 2.95.

4. See Alethea Hayter, *Mrs. Browning: A Poet's Work and Its Setting* (London: Faber, 1962), 105. Dorothy Mermin discusses this tendency in "The Female Poet and the Embarrassed Reader: Elizabeth Barrett Browning's *Sonnets from the Portuguese*," *ELH* 48.2 (1981): 351–67

5. Hayter, 105.

6. Laura Haigwood, "Gender-to-Gender Anxiety and Influence in Robert Browning's *Men and Women*," *Browning Institute Studies* 14 (1986): 108.

7. See, for example, Hayter, 105; Joanne Feit Diehl, "'Come slowly—Eden': An Exploration of Women Poets and Their Muse," *Signs* 3.3 (1978): 584.

8. Review of *Poems* (1862), *The Eclectic Review* 2 (1862): 205.

9. Review of *Poems* (1862), *Blackwood's Magazine* 91 (1862): 450.

10. R. H. Horne, *A New Spirit of the Age* (London: Oxford University Press, 1907), 338–39.

11. *Letters RB/EBB*, 1.13.

12. Daniel Karlin, *The Courtship of Robert Browning and Elizabeth Barrett* (Oxford: Clarendon, 1985), 256.

13. Karlin, 257.

14. Angela Leighton, *Elizabeth Barrett Browning* (Bloomington: Indiana University Press, 1986), 7–8.

15. Leighton, 94, 100.

16. Dorothy Mermin, "The Female Poet and the Embarrassed Reader" 352, 353.

17. Quotations from the *Sonnets* (vol. 3 of the *Complete Works*) are documented by sonnet number.

18. Luce Irigaray, *This Sex Which Is Not One*, trans. Catherine Porter with Carolyn Burke, (Ithaca: Cornell University Press, 1985), 25–26. See also Ellen Moers: "While so much male love poetry celebrates the glance of an eye, woman's love poems thrive on the touch, which is sometimes violent." *Literary Women* (New York: Doubleday, 1976), 169. My discussion of the difference between male and female lyric is indebted to Margaret Homans, "'Syllables of Velvet': Dickinson, Rossetti, and the Rhetorics of Sexuality," *Feminist Studies* 11.3 (1985): 569–93.

19. Barrett Browning is, of course, writing of gratified, not frustrated, desire, and the tactual image is also more appropriate in this context. But since she continues to emphasize tactual images in such subsequent works as *Aurora Leigh*, her use of these images in the *Sonnets* is not likely to be simply a matter of choosing an appropriate image for a particular situation.

20. There is also an interesting rejection of the visual here, a rejection of the *look* which would define her solely in the unacceptable role of passive beloved.

21. Hayter, 105.

22. Carol McGinnis Kay, "An Analysis of Sonnet 6 in *Sonnets from the Portuguese*," *Concerning Poetry* 4.1 (1971): 17–21.

23. Hayter, 105.

24. Stendhal, *On Love*, trans. Philip Sidney Woolf and Cecil N. Sidney Woolf (New York: Peter Pauper, n.d.), 31, 15.

25. For a discussion of the significance of hair in nineteenth-century literature, see Elizabeth Gitter, "The Power of Women's Hair in the Victorian Imagination," *PMLA* 99.5 (1984): 936–54.

26. See Karlin 271; Shaakeh Agajanian, *"Sonnets from the Portuguese" and the Love Sonnet Tradition* (New York: Philosophical Library, 1985), 93.

27. The sly and humorous quality of the tone in this poem is discussed by Leighton, 107–8.

28. Leighton, 101.

Chapter 5

1. On the subject of genre see Susan Friedman, "Gender and Genre Anxiety: Elizabeth Barrett Browning and H. D. as Epic Poets," *Tulsa Studies in Women's Literature* 5.2 (1986): 203–28; Dorothy Mermin, "Genre and Gender in *Aurora Leigh,*" *Victorian Newsletter* 69 (1986): 7–11; Marjorie Stone, "Genre Subversion and Gender Inversion: *The Princess* and *Aurora Leigh,*" *Victorian Poetry* 25.2 (1987): 101–27.

2. Quotations from *Aurora Leigh* (vols. 4, 5 of *Complete Works*) are cited by book and line number.

3. This is possibly one reason why Barrett Browning considered love and marriage more necessary for a man than for a woman (MRM 3.394); love can provide men with the emotional qualities women already possess.

4. Angela Leighton, *Elizabeth Barrett Browning* (Bloomington: Indiana University Press, 1986), 120.

5. Alethea Hayter, *Mrs. Browning: A Poet's Work and Its Setting* (London: Faber, 1962), 105, 171.

6. As Helen Cooper notes, "Aurora writes of these women through patriarchal eyes: Lady Waldemar is neither as monstrous nor Marian as angelic as Aurora fictionalizes them." *Elizabeth Barrett Browning, Woman and Artist* (Chapel Hill: University of Carolina Press, 1988), 157.

7. Mary Wollstonecraft, *A Vindication of the Rights of Women,* ed. Carol H. Poston (New York: Norton, 1975), 34.

8. Gardner Taplin, *The Life of Elizabeth Barrett Browning* (New Haven: Yale University Press, 1957), 340–41.

9. Review of *Aurora Leigh, Blackwood's Magazine* 81 (1857): 33.

10. Barrett Browning repeatedly speaks with admiration of women who possess what she sees as a masculine intellect. Harriet Martineau she called the "most manlike woman in the three kingdoms—in the best sense of the man—a woman gifted with admirable fortitude, as well as exercised in high logic, a woman of sensibility and of imagination certainly, but apt to carry her reason unbent wherever she sets her foot; given to utilitarian philosophy and the habit of logical analysis" (EBB 1.196–97).

11. See Sandra Donaldson, "Elizabeth Barrett's Two Sonnets to George Sand," *Studies in Browning and His Circle* 5.1 (1977): 21.

12. Nina Auerbach, "Robert Browning's Last Word," *Victorian Poetry* 22.2 (1984): 168.

13. *Blackwood's Magazine,* 33.

14. Friedman, 219.

15. Sandra Gilbert notes that Romney is afflicted by a self-division similar to that which affects Aurora. "That Romney craves a union with both social and sexual others is," Gilbert says, "a sign that, like Aurora, he is half consciously struggling toward a psychic reunification." "From *Patria* to *Matria*: Elizabeth Barrett Browning's Risorgimento," *PMLA* 99.2 (1984): 202.

16. Gilbert, 196.

17. Barbara Charlesworth Gelpi, "*Aurora Leigh:* The Vocation of the Woman Poet." *Victorian Poetry* 19.1 (1981): 46.

18. Review of *Aurora Leigh, Athenaeum* November 1856: 1425.

19. Kathleen Blake, *Love and the Woman Question in Victorian Literature: The Art of Self-Postponement* (Sussex: Harvester, 1983), 188.

20. Gelpi, 48.

21. Elaine Showalter, *A Literature of Their Own: British Women Novelists from Brontë to Lessing* (Princeton: Princeton University Press, 1977), 150.

22. Dolores Rosenblum, "Face to Face: Elizabeth Barrett Browning's *Aurora Leigh* and Nineteenth-Century Poetry," *Victorian Studies* 26.3 (1983): 335.

23. Mermin, 7.

24. Friedman, 219.

25. Merideth Raymond, "Elizabeth Barrett Browning's Poetics, 1845–1856: 'The Ascending Gyre,'" *Browning Society Notes* 11.2 (1981): 4.

Chapter 6

1. Gardner Taplin, *The Life of Elizabeth Barrett Browning* (New Haven: Yale University Press, 1957), 348.

2. Alethea Hayter, *Mrs. Browning: A Poet's Work and Its Setting* (London: Faber, 1962), 222–23.

3. Similarities in phrases used in this poem and Barrett Browning's letters about Sophia Eckley have prompted Hayter to conclude that the poem reveals Barrett Browning's response to Sophia (*Mrs. Browning,* 224). This would, of course, change the reading of the poem. (See my discussion of "Where's Agnes?") I do not think, however, that the poem gives any indication that the woman described is not as sweet as she appears, and consequently only biographical evidence could support this alternate reading. As in the case of "Where's Agnes?", the genesis of the poem may lie in Barrett Browning's experiences with Sophia, but, if so, she has radically transformed the situation.

4. Isobel Armstrong, ed., *Robert Browning* (Athens, Ohio: Ohio University Press, 1975), 275.

5. *Dearest Isa: Robert Browning's Letters to Isabella Blagden,* ed. Edward C. McAleer (Westport, Conn.: Greenwood, 1970), 35.

6. *Dearest Isa,* 295.

7. "New Letters from Mrs. Browning to Isa Blagden," ed. Edward C. McAleer, *PMLA* 66 (1951): 609.

8. *Dearest Isa,* 295.

9. *Dearest Isa,* 314.

10. Lord Walter's wife has shown that talk of "crimes irresistible" is "frivolous cant," and Barrett Browning seems to agree. One of her comments on George Sand is relevant in this context: "The dangerous point in George Sand, appears to me to lie in the *irresistible* power she attributes to human passion. The *moral* of *Jacques*—to apply such a term to the most immoral

of lessons,...is just that Love, guilty love, observe,...cannot be resisted by the strongest will and the most virtuous individuality" (MRM 2.462). Barrett Browning clearly believes it can be resisted and that Guilio is a poor specimen, quite undeserving of Bianca's devotion.

11. This is reminiscent of elder sister's claim that she cannot hold Robert responsible for preferring the youth and beauty of Bertha.

Bibliography

Primary Sources: Poetry

"Aurora Leigh" and Other Poems. Intro. Cora Kaplan. London: Women's Press, 1978.
The Complete Works of Elizabeth Barrett Browning. Ed. Charlotte Porter and Helen A. Clarke. 6 vols. New York: Crowell, 1900; AMS Reprint, 1973.
Elizabeth Barrett Browning: Hitherto Unpublished Poems and Stories with an Inedited Autobiography. Intro. H. Buxton Forman. 2 vols. Boston: Bibliophile, 1914.
"Fragment of An 'Essay on Woman.'" *Studies in Browning and His Circle* 12 (1984): 11–12.
New Poems by Robert Browning and Elizabeth Barrett Browning. Ed. Sir Frederic Kenyon. London: Smith, 1914.
The Poet's Enchiridion. Ed. H. Buxton Forman. Boston: Bibliophile, 1914.
A Variorum Edition of Elizabeth Barrett Browning's Sonnets from the Portuguese. Ed. Miroslava Wein Dow. New York: Whitson, 1980.

Primary Sources: Letters and Other Writings

Dearest Isa: Robert Browning's Letters to Isabella Blagden. Ed. Edward C. McAleer. Westport, Conn.: Greenwood, 1970.
Diary by E. B. B.: The Unpublished Diary of Elizabeth Barrett Barrett, 1831–1832. Ed. Philip Kelley and Ronald Hudson. Athens, Ohio: Ohio University Press, 1969.
Elizabeth Barrett to Mr. Boyd. Ed. Barbara P. McCarthy. London: John Murray, 1955.
Elizabeth Barrett Browning: Letters to Her Sister, 1846–1859. Ed. Leonard Huxley. London: Murray, 1929.
Elizabeth Barrett Browning's Letters to Mrs. David Ogilvy: 1849–1861. Ed. Peter N. Heydon and Philip Kelley. New York: Quadrangle, 1973.
Invisible Friends: The Correspondence of Elizabeth Barrett Barrett and Benjamin Robert Haydon, 1842–1845. Ed. Willard Bissell Pope. Cambridge: Harvard University Press, 1972.
Letters of the Brownings to George Barrett. Ed. Paul Landis with Ronald E. Freeman. Urbana: University of Illinois Press, 1958.
The Letters of Elizabeth Barrett Browning. Ed. Frederic G. Kenyon. 2 vols. London: Smith, 1887.
Letters of Elizabeth Barrett Browning Addressed to Richard Hengist Horne. Ed. S. Mayer. New York: Knox, 1877.
The Letters of Elizabeth Barrett Browning to Mary Russell Mitford: 1836–1854. Ed. Meredith B. Raymond and Mary Rose Sullivan. 3 vols. Waco, Tex.: Armstrong Browning Library, 1983.
The Letters of Robert Browning and Elizabeth Barrett Barrett: 1845–1846. Ed. Elvan Kintner. 2 vols. Cambridge, Mass.: Harvard University Press, 1969.

"New Letters from Mrs. Browning to Isa Blagden." Ed. Edward C. McAleer. *PMLA* 66 (1951): 594–612.

Twenty-two Unpublished Letters of Elizabeth Barrett Browning and Robert Browning Addressed to Henrietta and Arabella Moulton-Barrett. New York: United Features, 1935.

"Two Autobiographical Essays by Elizabeth Barrett." *Browning Institute Studies* 2 (1974): 119–34.

Reviews

The Seraphim, and Other Poems (1838)
   Athenaeum July 7 1838: 466–68.
   Blackwood's Magazine 44 (1838): 279–84. ["Christopher North"].
   Metropolitan Magazine 22 (1838): 97–101.
   Quarterly Review 66 (1840): 382–89.

Poems (1844)
   Athenaeum August 24 1844: 763–64. [Henry Chorley].
   Atlas August 31 1844: 593–94.
   Blackwood's Magazine 56 (1844): 621–39.
   Broadway Journal January 1845: 1–2, 4–8, 17–20. Reviewed under American title of *The Drama of Exile and Other Poems.* [Edgar Allan Poe].
   Examiner October 5 1844: 627–29. [John Forster].
   New Monthly Magazine 72 (1844): 282–84.
   Prospective Review 1 (1845): 445–64.
   Westminster Review 42 (1844): 381–92.

Poems (1850)
   Athenaeum November 1850: 1242–44. [Henry Chorley].
   Eclectic Review 93 (1851): 295–303.
   Fraser's Magazine 43 (1851): 178–82.
   Guardian January 1851: 55–56.
   Spectator January 1851: 85–86.

Aurora Leigh (1856)
   Athenaeum November 1856: 1425–27.
   Blackwood's Magazine 81 (1857): 23–41.
   Dublin University Magazine 49 (1857): 460–70.
   Literary Gazette November 1856: 917–18.
   North British Review 26 (1857): 443–62. [Coventry Patmore].
   Spectator 29 (1856): 1239–40.
   Westminster Review 68 (1857): 399–415.

Poems (1862)
   Blackwood's Magazine 91 (1862): 449–51.
   Eclectic Review 2 (1862): 189–212.
   Saturday Review 13 (1862): 472–74.

Last Poems (1862)
   Athenaeum March 1862: 421–22. [Henry Chorley].
   Christian Examiner 72 (1862): 65–88.

Dublin University Magazine 60 (1862): 157–62.
North British Review 36 (1862): 514–34. [Coventry Patmore].

Secondary Sources

Agajanian, Shaakeh S. *Sonnets from the Portuguese and the Love Sonnet Tradition.* New York: Philosophical Library, 1985.

Armstrong, Isobel, ed. *Robert Browning.* Athens, Ohio: Ohio University Press, 1975.

Auerbach, Nina. "Robert Browning's Last Word." *Victorian Poetry* 22.2 (1984): 161–73.

Ball, Patricia M. *The Heart's Events: The Victorian Poetry of Relationships.* London: Athlone, 1976.

Berridge, Elizabeth. "A Talk on *Aurora Leigh.*" *Browning Society Notes* 7.2 (1977): 73–81.

Blake, Kathleen. "Elizabeth Barrett Browning and Wordsworth: The Romantic Poet as a Woman." *Victorian Poetry* 24.4 (1986): 387–398.

_____ . *Love and the Woman Question in Victorian Literature: The Art of Self-Postponement.* Sussex: Harvester, 1983.

Boas, Louise. *Elizabeth Barrett Browning.* New York: Longman, 1930.

Broadbent, J. B. *Poetic Love* London: Chatto, 1964.

Browning, Robert. *Poetical Works. 1833–1864.* Ed. Ian Jack. Oxford: Oxford University Press, 1970.

Burdett, Osbert. *The Brownings.* London: Constable, 1928.

Castan, C. "Structural Problems and the Poetry of *Aurora Leigh.*" *Browning Society Notes* 7.3 (1977): 53–58.

Chaucer, Geoffrey. *The Works of Geoffrey Chaucer.* Ed. F. N. Robinson. Boston: Houghton, 1957.

Clarke, Isobel C. *Elizabeth Barrett Browning: A Portrait.* New York: Kenikat, 1970.

Cooper, Helen. *Elizabeth Barrett Browning, Woman and Artist.* Chapel Hill: University of North Carolina Press, 1988.

_____ . "Working Into Light: Elizabeth Barrett Browning." *Shakespeare's Sisters: Feminist Essays on Women Poets.* Ed. Sandra M. Gilbert and Susan Gubar. Bloomington: Indiana University Press, 1979. 65–81.

David, Deirdre. "'Art's a Service': Social Wound, Sexual Politics, and *Aurora Leigh.*" *Browning Institute Studies* 13 (1985): 113–36.

_____ . *Intellectual Women and Victorian Patriarchy: Harriet Martineau, Elizabeth Barrett Browning, George Eliot.* New York: Cornell University Press, 1987.

DeJean, Joan. "Fictions of Sappho." *Critical Inquiry* 13.4 (1987): 787–805.

Diehl, Joanne Feit. "'Come Slowly—Eden': An Exploration of Women Poets and Their Muse." *Signs* 3.3 (1978): 572–87.

Donaldson, Sandra. "Elizabeth Barrett's Two Sonnets to George Sand." *Studies in Browning and His Circle* 5.1 (1977): 19–22.

_____ . "'Motherhood's Advent in Power': Elizabeth Barrett Browning's Poems About Motherhood." *Victorian Poetry* 18.1 (1980): 51–60.

Donne, John. *The Complete English Poems.* Ed. A. J. Smith. New York: Penguin, 1971.

Field, Kate. "Elizabeth Barrett Browning." *Atlantic Monthly* 8.47 (1861): 368–76.

Friedman, Susan Stanford. "Gender and Genre Anxiety: Elizabeth Barrett Browning and H. D. as Epic Poets." *Tulsa Studies in Women's Literature* 5.2 (1986): 203–28.

Fuller, Margaret. *Papers on Literature and Art.* London: Wiley, 1846.

Gelpi, Barbara Charlesworth. "*Aurora Leigh:* The Vocation of the Woman Poet." *Victorian Poetry* 19.1 (1981): 35–48.

Gilbert, Sandra M. "From *Patria* to *Matria:* Elizabeth Barrett Browning's Risorgimento." *PMLA* 99.2 (1984): 194–211.

Gilbert, Sandra M., and Susan Gubar. *The Madwoman in the Attic.* New Haven: Yale University Press, 1979.

Gitter, Elizabeth G. "The Power of Women's Hair in the Victorian Imagination." *PMLA* 99.5 (1984): 936–54.

Going, William T. "Elizabeth Barrett Browning's *Sonnets from the Portuguese* 43." *Examiner* 11.8 (1953): Item 58.

Green, Roger Lancelyn, ed. *A Book of British Ballads.* London: Dent, 1966.

Haigwood, Laura E. "Gender-to-Gender Anxiety and Influence in Robert Browning's *Men and Women.*" *Browning Institute Studies* 14 (1986): 97–118.

Hale, S. J., ed. *The Ladies' Wreath.* Boston: Marsh, 1837.

Hayter, Alethea. *Mrs. Browning: A Poet's Work and Its Setting.* London: Faber, 1962.

———. "'These Men Over-Nice': Elizabeth Barrett Browning's 'Lord Walter's Wife.'" *Browning Society Notes* 8.2 (1978): 5–7.

Heilman, Robert B. "Elizabeth Barrett Browning's *Sonnets from the Portuguese* 43." *Examiner* 4.1 (1945): Item 3.

Hemans, Felicia. *The Poetical Works of Mrs. Hemans.* London: Warne, n.d.

Herbert, George. *The English Poems of George Herbert.* Ed. C. A. Patrides. London: Dent, 1974.

Hewlett, Dorothy. *Elizabeth Barrett Browning: A Life.* New York: Knopf, 1952.

Hickok, Kathleen K. "'New Yet Orthodox'—The Female Characters in *Aurora Leigh.*" *International Journal of Women's Studies* 3.5 (1980): 479–89.

———. *Representations of Women: Nineteenth-Century British Women's Poetry.* Westport, Conn.: Greenwood, 1984.

Hicks, Malcolm. "Elizabeth Barrett Browning's 'Lord Walter's Wife': Its Family History." *Browning Society Notes* 8.3 (1978): 7–12.

Holloway, Julia Bolton. "*Aurora Leigh* and *Jane Eyre.*" *Brontë Society Transactions* 17 (1977): 126–32.

Homans, Margaret. "'Syllables of Velvet': Dickinson, Rossetti, and the Rhetorics of Sexuality." *Feminist Studies* 11.3 (1985): 569–93.

———. *Women Writers and Poetic Identity: Dorothy Wordsworth, Emily Brontë, and Emily Dickinson.* Princeton: Princeton University Press, 1980.

Horne, R. H. *A New Spirit of the Age.* London: Oxford University Press, 1907.

Ingram, John H. *Elizabeth Barrett Browning.* Boston: Roberts, 1888.

Irigaray, Luce. *This Sex Which is Not One.* Trans. Catherine Porter with Carolyn Burke. Ithaca: Cornell University Press, 1985.

Johnson, Wendell Stacy. *Sex and Marriage in Victorian Poetry.* Ithaca: Cornell University Press, 1975.

Karlin, Daniel. *The Courtship of Robert Browning and Elizabeth Barrett.* Oxford: Clarendon, 1985.

Kay, Carol McGinnis. "An Analysis of Sonnet 6 in *Sonnets from the Portuguese.*" *Concerning Poetry* 4.1 (1971): 17–21.

Kelley, Philip, and Betty A. Coley. *The Browning Collections: A Reconstruction with Other Memorabilia.* Waco, Tex.: Armstrong Browning Library, 1984.

Landon, Letitia E. *Poetical Works.* 2 vols. London: Longman, 1853.

———. "The Secret Discovered," *Friendship's Offering* (1837): 320–24.

———. *The Venetian Bracelet and Other Poems.* London: Longman, 1829.

Leighton, Angela. *Elizabeth Barrett Browning.* Bloomington: Indiana University Press, 1986.

Letzring, Monica. "Strangford's *Poems from the Portuguese of Luis de Camoens.*" *Comparative Literature* 23.4 (1971): 289–311.

Lipking, Lawrence. "Aristotle's Sister: A Poetics of Abandonment." *Critical Inquiry* 10.1 (1983): 61–81.

Lupton, Mary Jane. *Elizabeth Barrett Browning.* New York: Feminist Press, 1972.

Mander, Rosalie. *Mrs. Browning: The Story of Elizabeth Barrett.* London: Weidenfeld, 1980.

Marks, Jeannette. *The Family of the Barretts: A Colonial Romance.* New York: MacMillan, 1938.

Meredith, Michael. "The Wounded Heroine: Elizabeth Barrett's Sophocles." *Studies in Browning and His Circle* 3.2 (1975): 1–12.

Mermin, Dorothy. "Barrett Browning's Stories." *Browning Institute Studies* 13 (1985): 99–112.

———. "The Damsel, the Knight, and the Victorian Woman Poet." *Critical Inquiry* 13.1 (1986): 64–80.

———. "The Domestic Economy of Art: Elizabeth Barrett and Robert Browning." *Mothering the Mind: Twelve Studies of Writers and Their Silent Partners.* Ed. Ruth Perry and Martine Wetson Brownley. New York: Holmes, 1984.

———. "Elizabeth Barrett Browning through 1844: Becoming a Woman Poet." *Studies in English Literature* 26.4 (1986): 713–36.

———. "The Female Poet and the Embarrassed Reader: Elizabeth Barrett Browning's *Sonnets from the Portuguese.*" *ELH* 48.2 (1981): 351–67.

———. "Genre and Gender in *Aurora Leigh.*" *Victorian Newsletter* 69 (1986): 7–11.

[Mitford, Mary Russell.] *Findens' Tableaux of National Character, Beauty, and Costume.* 2 vols. Reprint. London: March, 1843.

Mitford, Mary Russell. *The Life of Mary Russell Mitford: Told by Herself in Letters to Her Friends.* Ed. Rev. A. G. K. L'Estrange. 2 vols. New York: Harper, 1870. Vol. 2.

Moers, Ellen. *Literary Women.* New York: Doubleday, 1976.

Monteiro, George. "On First Looking into Strangford's Camoes: Elizabeth Barrett Browning's 'Catarina to Camoens.'" *Studies in Browning and His Circle* 8 (1980): 7–19.

———. "The Presence of Camoes in Elizabeth Barrett Browning's *Sonnets from the Portuguese.*" *Browning Society Notes* 12 (1982): 19–21.

Moser, Kay. "Elizabeth Barrett's Youthful Feminism: Fragment of 'An Essay on Woman.'" *Studies in Browning and His Circle* 12 (1984): 13–26.

———. "The Victorian Critics' Dilemma: What to Do with a Talented Poetess?" *Victorians Institute Journal* 13 (1985): 59–66.

Mulock, Dinah. *Thirty Years: Being Poems, New and Old.* Boston: Houghton, n.d.

Paroissien, David. "Mrs. Browning's Influence on and Contribution to *A New Spirit of the Age.*" *English Language Notes* 8.3 (1970): 274–81.

Patmore, Coventry. *The Angel in the House.* 2 vols. London: MacMillan, 1863.

Peters, John Gerard. "Love, Heaven, and Human Existence: A Note on Elizabeth Barrett Browning's 'Sonnet 22.'" *Studies in Browning and His Circle* 12 (1984): 32–33.

Phillipson, John S. "'How Do I Love Thee?'—An Echo of St. Paul." *Victorian Newsletter* 22 (1962): 22.

Poe, Edgar Allan. "The Philosophy of Composition." *The Complete Poems and Stories of Edgar Allan Poe, with Selections from his Critical Writings,* ed. A. H. Quinn. New York: Knopf, 1951. Vol. 2.

Radley, Virginia. *Elizabeth Barrett Browning.* New York: Twayne, 1972.

Raymond, Meredith. "Elizabeth Barrett's Early Poetics: The 1820s." *Browning Society Notes* 8.3 (1978): 3–7.

———. "Elizabeth Barrett Browning's Poetics, 1830–1844: 'The Seraph and the Earthly Piper.'" *Browning Society Notes* 9.1 (1979): 5–9.

———. "Elizabeth Barrett Browning's Poetics, 1845–1856: 'The Ascending Gyre.'" *Browning Society Notes* 11.2 (1981): 1–11.

Ridenour, George. "Robert Browning and *Aurora Leigh.*" *Victorian Newsletter* 67 (1985): 26–31.

Robertson, Eric. *English Poetesses.* London: Cassell, 1883.

Roscoe, William Caldwell. *Poems and Essays.* Ed. Richard Hutton. 2 vols. London: Chapman Hall, 1860.

Rosenblum, Dolores. "Casa Guidi Windows and *Aurora Leigh.*" *Tulsa Studies in Women's Literature* 4.1 (1985): 61–68.

———— . *Christina Rossetti: The Poetry of Endurance.* Carbondale: Southern Illinois University Press, 1986.

———— . "Face to Face: Elizabeth Barrett Browning's *Aurora Leigh* and Nineteenth-Century Poetry." *Victorian Studies* 26.3 (1983): 321–38.

Rougemont, Denis de. *Love in the Western World.* Trans. Montgomery Belgion. New York: Pantheon, 1956.

Ruskin, John. "Of Queens' Gardens." *Sesame and Lilies.* London: Dent, 1911. 48–79.

Sandstrom, Glenn. "'James Lee's Wife'—and Browning's." *Victorian Poetry* 4 (1966): 259–70.

Shackford, Martha Hale. *Studies of Certain Nineteenth-Century Poets.* Natick, Mass.: Suburban, 1946.

Shakespeare, William. *Shakespeare's Sonnets.* Ed. Louis B. Wright and Virginia A. LaMar. New York: Simon, 1967.

Shapiro, Marianne. "The Provençal Trobairitz and the Limits of Courtly Love." *Signs* 3.3 (1978): 560–71.

Sharp, Phillip David. *Poetry in Process: Elizabeth Barrett Browning and the Sonnets Notebook.* Diss. Louisiana State University, 1985.

Showalter, Elaine. *A Literature of Their Own: British Women Novelists from Brontë to Lessing.* Princeton: Princeton University Press, 1977.

Singer, Irving. *The Nature of Love.* 2 vols. Chicago: University of Chicago Press, 1984.

Stanley, Hiram M. "The Browning-Barrett Love Letters and the Psychology of Love." *Open Court* 13 (1899): 731–41.

Stedman, Edmund Clarence. *Victorian Poets.* Boston: Houghton, 1891.

Steinmetz, Virginia. "Beyond the Sun: Patriarchal Images in *Aurora Leigh.*" *Studies in Browning and His Circle* 9.2 (1981): 18–41.

———— . "Images of 'Mother Want' in Elizabeth Barrett Browning's *Aurora Leigh.*" *Victorian Poetry* 21.4 (1983): 351–67.

Stendhal [Henri Beyle]. *On Love.* Trans. Philip Sidney Woolf and Cecil N. Sidney Woolf. New York: Peter Pauper, n.d.

Stone, Marjorie. "Genre Subversion and Gender Inversion: *The Princess* and *Aurora Leigh.*" *Victorian Poetry* 25.2 (1987): 101–27.

———— . "Taste, Totems, and Taboos: The Female Breast in Victorian Poetry." *Dalhousie Review* 64.4 (1984): 748–70.

Strangford, Lord Viscount. *Poems, from the Portuguese of Luis de Camoens.* London: Carpenter, 1805.

Taplin, Gardner. *The Life of Elizabeth Barrett Browning.* New Haven: Yale University Press, 1957.

Tennyson, Alfred Lord. *Tennyson's Poetry.* Ed. Robert W. Hill, Jr. New York: Norton, 1971.

Thomson, Patricia. *George Sand and the Victorians.* London: MacMillan, 1977.

Whiting, Lilian. *A Study of Elizabeth Barrett Browning.* London: Gay, 1899.

Wollstonecraft, Mary. *A Vindication of the Rights of Women.* Ed. Carol H. Poston. New York: Norton, 1975.

Woolf, Virginia. *The Common Reader, Second Series.* London: Hogarth, 1932.

Woolford, John. "EBB: the Natural and the Spiritual." *Browning Society Notes* 8.1 (1978): 15–19.

———— . "EBB: 'Woman and Poet.'" *Browning Society Notes* 9.3 (1979): 3–5.

Zimmerman, Susan. "*Sonnets from the Portuguese:* A Negative and a Positive Context." *Mary Wollstonecraft Newsletter* 2.1 (1973): 7–20.

Index